IMPORTANT

The nutritional information in this book is approximate and based on each recipe before additional options are incorporated.

Fitness photo: Liana Louzon
BGHL lifestyle photos: Amy Wagner
Food photography: Istock photo, Lori Harder, Veer
Cover design: Chelsea Klevesahl
Cookbook editing, design and layout: Heidi Zeto

contents

about the author

As Lori Harder's debut cookbook title suggests, Lori truly is a Busy Girl leading a Healthy Life. Lori is an expert trainer, fitness model, motivational speaker, cookbook author, and wellness and nutrition coach. She owns and operates multiple businesses while juggling a healthy lifestyle, travel and a happy family life. Setting records in her field, Lori also is a three-time national fitness title-holder, including the 2010 Miss Bikini Universe title.

Lori strives to be a healthy, motivational role model to others and at all times, be camera ready. She wants everyone to experience the same amount of happiness, energy and success that comes from feeding your body the healthy (good-tasting) foods it needs to function well.

"I refuse to sacrifice taste and my social life," Lori says. "I really believe you can have it all with a little creativity, proper education, preparation and nutrition! If you put great things in your body," your body will perform the way it was intended to, and you will feel and look amazing! Our body is a miracle and when you take care of it, it will take care of you."

Lori lives in Minnesota with her husband, Chris and her dog, Waffles.
They enjoy being active year-round with a daily run or walk around the local lakes.

special thanks

There are so many people who make my life more blessed than I deserve, so I would like to take a moment to name a few who have made this book possible...

To my mother-in-law, Marie, this would still just be a dream without your brilliance in the kitchen. Thank you for all of your support and hard work on so many recipes and in everything we do. And thank you for seeing the vision and pouring your heart into all of our recipes.

Thanks to my amazing husband and best friend for all of your support in everything I do. The fact that you believe in me makes me feel like I can do anything. Thanks for being my sounding board, taste-tester and partner in dreaming!

Thanks to my mom and dad for teaching me to cook and get creative! I will never forget the memories of hanging out in the kitchen and cooking together. Dad, thanks for eating my entire batch of "cinnamon and sugar cookies" that were actually "cumin and sugar cookies," just so I wouldn't feel bad. And to my mom, I'm sorry that I lied to you about eating all four blueberry muffins. "No mom, I just saw them! They have to be in here somewhere!" It was only because you were such a good cook, and I couldn't resist!

Looking back, it's obvious that my creativity in the kitchen comes from both my mom and dad. Many of my childhood memories revolve around my family cooking together and bonding over great food. My dad even built a separate mini counter for my sister and I so we could cook, too. My parents also made me try at least a bite of everything. They would say, "How on Earth will you know if you don't like it if you never try it?" And so with those words echoing in my brain, down the hatch everything went! I learned not to fear anything when it came to food!

Unfortunately, this "fearlessness" led me down a path of overindulgence. Even as a young kid, I noticed that I felt tired and lethargic from continually eating junk. And what's worse, my clothes started to fit tighter. I knew I had to do something about it. But how was I — a self-proclaimed lover of all foods — going to get in shape and feel better when I had no clue how to begin? And so, my lifelong search for knowledge about health and nutrition began. I was determined to find a way to make healthy meals taste incredible for everyone — especially myself.

Fast forward a whole lot of years, and a lot of trial and error in the healthy cooking department, and the Busy Girl Healthy Life™ idea was born. I will never forget the day the light-bulb moment happened. I was sitting around the table with my husband and mother-in-law eating a delicious, healthy meal. I was rambling on about how I wanted to share my knowledge (and love) with others about staying fit and keeping balance in life despite being crazy busy. Finally, after a lot of back and forth on how I could accomplish this, my mother-in-law, Marie, and I realized we had a great thing to share. Yep, you guessed it — Busy Girl Healthy Life. With the combination of her hearty home-style cooking background and my healthy, creative background, we have made it our mission to come up with the most delicious, quick and healthy recipes to prove we can fool anyone into eating healthy! [Insert evil laugh here...]

Busy Girl Healthy Life was created out of a desire to be healthy, feel great, look great and have energy — without compromising the taste of food (or the size of your waistline). I know first-hand that if I don't eat healthy food, I won't have the energy to live the life I want. Eating healthy food is truly the secret to staying motivated and energized. And, I want everyone to share this feeling!

Busy Girl Healthy Life recipes are versatile enough that you can eat them at home, take them on the go or make for parties or guests. These foods will keep you feeling energized, full and happy while keeping taste buds content!

Ready to find out for yourself? Set your timers, take control of your health and get ready to enjoy some family favorites sure to please even the toughest food critic! I hope you love these recipes as much as I loved creating them.

Bon appétit!

a note from the author

Hi there!

I just wanted to take the time to say hello and express my deepest gratitude to you for picking up my cookbook. I hope it takes you on an amazing journey of discovery as you start your new healthy way of life! I also wanted to give an extra special thanks to those who have supported Busy Girl Healthy Life for the last couple years. You have given me an outlet to be creative, and I can't tell you how rewarding it is to see my visions and dreams become a reality. Without all of you this would still be just a wish.

When you feel great, you have the energy to get done all that your busy life entails. Processed foods rob of us of so much more than just our confidence in our bodies. They rob us of our time, energy and happiness. This new way of eating and living will change the way you feel about healthy food. When we eat real food, we start to feel and look the way we were intended to — AMAZING!

As a former overweight child turned fitness cover model, I have dedicated my life to living healthy. But this cookbook represents so much more than healthy recipes. It represents my journey and my passion to feel good, get fit and stay fit — all while balancing life's everyday happenings. I want to share this message of balance and feeling incredible with everyone.

These recipes are fast, tasty and easy! And they get their flavor from fruits, veggies, proteins and incredible spices — just the way we were meant to eat! No matter how active you are, your hard work won't show without a consistent healthy diet. Busy Girl Healthy Life makes it easy by taking the guesswork out of meal planning. The recipes are balanced and include the building blocks for a healthy body and happy brain. And who doesn't want that?

Thank you again for joining me on this journey. I hope my books will be a part of your life's greatest memories for a long time to come. Please don't hesitate to let me know your thoughts — you are the heart of Busy Girl Healthy Life!

Lori Harder
Busy Girl

busy girl healthy life's top 25 spices

One of the most common things I hear from the busy girl trying to cook a healthy and good tasting meal is that they never seem to have the spices or herbs that are called for in a recipe. Herbs and spices are the best way to add a TON of incredible flavor with hardly any calories. So here it is, the 25 spices and herbs every cook should keep in their pantry:

1. BASIL (Dried) Common seasoning for meat, fish, tomato dishes, pizza sauce, soups, stews, dressings and salads.

2. CAYENNE PEPPER (Ground) Also called red pepper. Most commonly used in Mexican and Italian dishes, Indian foods, chili products, sausage, salsas, dressings and relishes. A very strong spice so must be used in moderation.

3. CELERY (Seed or Flakes) Used in stews, soups, fish dishes, salads & dressings, and veggie dishes.

4. CHILI POWDER Commonly used in Mexican foods, sauces (such as barbecue & taco sauce) chili's, marinades and dips. This is quite spicy and should be used in moderation.

5. CHIVES (Dried or can be chopped & frozen) Have a light onion flavor and are commonly used to flavor dips, sauces, soups, egg dishes, baked potatoes, and veggie dishes. Can be used to replace onion flavor in a recipe. Chives are a good source of potassium, iron and calcium.

6. CINNAMON (Ground) Commonly used in spiced beverages, pudding, baked goods, sauces, some soups, meats, chicken, Chinese and Indian dishes.

7. CILANTRO (Dried) commonly used in Mexican dishes, salsas, salad dressings, and sauces. Don't over use in a recipe, people either love the flavor or hate it. Those that hate it say it tastes like dishwater.

8. CLOVES (Ground) This is a strong spice to be used in moderation in baked goods, ham, sweet potatoes, baked beans, puddings, soups, sausages and sauces such as barbecue.

9. CORIANDER (Ground) Has a sweet musk flavor. Commonly used Mexican dishes, cookies, cakes, biscuits, spiced dishes, cheese dishes, pea soup and pork.

10. CUMIN (Ground) Commonly used in Mexican dishes, curry dishes, chili's, soups, stews, and sauces. Has an unique and distinct flavor but really not spicy.

11. CURRY (Powder) This is a blend of at least 20 spices and herbs. Commonly used in Indian dishes, poultry, soups, stews, meat dishes and sauces.

12. DILL (Weed) Usually used cottage cheese, soups, chowders, salads, sauerkraut, potato salad, fish, meat sauces, dips and apple pie. Great in egg salad.

13. FENNEL (Seed) Commonly used in Italian sausage, pork dishes, fish dishes, squash, sweet pickles, cabbage, pastries, Italian dishes and pizza sauce.

14. GARLIC (Powder) Commonly used in hundreds of dishes, especially in Italian cooking, chicken, meat, fish, sauces, breads, dips and salads. Almost as commonly used as salt and pepper. When used in cooking always add the garlic towards the end because garlic burns very easily and may taste bitter. Also, a must have for the fridge is minced garlic.

15. *GINGER* (Ground) Has a pungent spicy flavor and is used in Oriental and Indian cooking. Also used in dressing, dried fruits, gingerbread and pumpkin pie. A little goes a long way.

16. *ITALIAN SEASONING* (Dried) This seasoning is a combination of marjoram, thyme, rosemary, savory, sage, oregano and basil. It is a perfect base for any Italian dish. Can be used on poultry, beef, fish, and meatloaf. It is great in sauces, dips, dressings, and on veggies. It is considered a good all-around seasoning.

17. *MARJORAM* (Dried) Part of the oregano family but with a sweet nutty flavor. It is usually combined with other herbs and used in potato dishes, soups, stews, poultry seasoning, sauces, Greek dishes, and fish dishes.

18. *NUTMEG* (Ground) A relatively sweet spice that adds that little something special to cheese dishes, soups, stews and creamed foods. Great sprinkle on top of custard, eggnog, and whipped cream. Also used in some sausages and ravioli. It boasts a somewhat strong flavor so should be used in moderation.

19. *ONION POWDER* This is often used in partnership with garlic powder. Can be used in dips, sauces, soups, stews, Italian dishes, Mexican dishes, and casseroles. Use in moderation.

20. *OREGANO* (Dried) Commonly used in Italian specialties such as spaghetti sauces, pizzas, soups, stews, tomatoes, and roasted root veggies. Sprinkle lightly on a grilled cheese sandwich, YUMMY!

21. *PAPRIKA* (Ground, Sweet) PAPRIKA (Ground, Smoky) Sweet paprika has a mild flavor and is commonly used in cream sauces, salad dressings, egg dishes, and veggie dishes. It is often used as a powder garnish. Smoky paprika has a spicier flavor and adds a hint: of smokiness to Mexican, Italian, and Indian dishes. Adds good flavor to spicy sauces (such as barbecue), ketchup, and sausages.

22. *RED PEPPER FLAKES* (Crushed) Spicy, Spicy, Spicy! Adds bold spicy flavor to pasta sauces, pizza, chili's and sauted veggies. Used in most Italian, Mexican and Asian dishes. Add a few flakes to sweet sauces and cheese dishes for that little something extra. The contrast is great and livens up the sweet and cheese dishes. Be careful when using this spice, it carries a kick!

23. *ROSEMARY* (Crushed) This is a sweet, spicy and fragrant herb with a pungent aroma. Commonly used in meat and poultry dishes, Italian dishes, dressings, soups, and stews.

24. *TARRAGON* (Dried) Has a flavor similar to licorice. Commonly used in sauces, meat, poultry, and fish dishes, salads, herb dressings and tomato casseroles. Has a very pleasant flavor and aroma.

25. *THYME* (Dried) This has a somewhat strong flavor commonly used in stews, tomato based soups and sauces, poultry, meats, sausages and chowders.

Well cooks, this is the Busy Girl's spice and herb bible. Don't get overwhelmed. You don't have to go out and buy them all immediately. Just take this list with you to the grocery store and pick up a few at a time. You can find small containers of these spices and herbs at reasonable prices (usually under $1!) in the spice aisle. Before you know it you will have your own spice pantry that can accommodate any recipe. If you find you do not have a specific spice called for in a recipe, chances are you will have a good substitute that will still enhance the recipe.

Have fun experimenting with your spices and herbs. Smell and taste your spices, and then try adding some to your favorite recipes. Just remember not to add too much of any one spice, easy does it in the beginning! Dried and ground herbs and spices are stronger than fresh ones, less expensive and last a lot longer.

Enjoy!

busy girl healthy life lifestyle tips & tricks

1. **Eat more often.** This keeps you from energy crashes, getting tired and making bad food choices. Aim to eat 5 to 6 small meals or 3 average meals and 2 snacks. You may need to work up to eating this often, but keep trying! This is a great way to ensure you'll never get too hungry and make choices that aren't in line with your goals.

2. **Always plan ahead!** Whether you're headed to a party or to the office, the only way to set yourself up in an environment for success is by planning ahead. You must have a plan at all times and bring healthy options whenever possible. Chances are, your friends and family will end up enjoying them, too!

3. **Keep the essentials on hand.** No matter how much planning we do, sometimes life gets in the way. Always keep a few of your favorite Busy Girl Healthy Life™ recipes frozen, individually wrapped, and ready to warm and eat!

4. **This is a lifestyle.** That means you must ease your way into it in order to make sure it's something you can stick with long term. Don't jump head-first and think you'll fall in love with it. Just like anything, change takes getting used to. Start with switching 1 to 2 of your meals each day the first week and add more as time goes on. Soon you'll feel great and start craving clean food all the time!

5. **Move more.** Exercise and muscle help shape your body and eating healthy will reveal it! Don't be afraid to lift some weights to keep your metabolism burning fat and calories. Make your body work for you even when you're not. I love to take a walk after a big meal or if I'm bored and can't seem to stop craving everything under the sun. This helps shift your mood and focus to something unrelated to food. Get your family or walking buddy to join you!

6. **Fill most of your plate with lean protein and veggies.** I don't believe in eliminating carbohydrates or fruit from your diet — EVER! Feeling deprived will always lead to binging. Fill up on veggies, fruits and proteins, and keep the other stuff in moderation.

7. **Make healthier versions of your favorites or keep your portion size small.** If you MUST have some chocolate or pizza, try to make a healthier version. If this doesn't quench the craving, drink a large glass of water and have a small serving of the real thing. Most times, we realize it wasn't as good as we imagined. This also helps keep you from feeling deprived. Remember, this is a lifestyle! If you think you'll never be able to have something again, you'll never feel this lifestyle is maintainable.

8. **Recruit your family and friends.** This is much easier and more fun when the whole family is on board! Ask them what they're in the mood for and see how tasty you can make a healthier version. Involve them and remind them of how great they feel when they eat healthy!

9. **Plan your weekends and vacations around activities.** Oftentimes, we plan our social events around food. This creates a very challenging environment to be healthy in, not to mention it's not a good lesson to teach our children. Try taking a class, a fun new lesson, playing games or heading outside for some family and friend time. There is nothing better than playing outside all day!

10. **Reward yourself with things that don't involve food or drink.** For most everything in our lives, we've rewarded ourselves with a celebration revolving around food and booze. As a result, when we do something good, we associate warm, fuzzy feelings with indulging. In turn, when we try to take the healthier path, we feel like we're missing out. Start celebrating your victories by treating yourself to a concert, ball game, massage, amusement park or a great new outfit!

breakfast

banana french toast sticks

Makes 2 servings (serving = about 5 sticks).

INGREDIENTS

3   slices Ezekiel® bread (or bread of your choice)
1   egg
1   egg white
1   tsp. vanilla
5   packets stevia or 3 Tbsp. sugar
3   Tbsp. low-fat buttermilk
½   banana
½   tsp. cinnamon

INSTRUCTIONS

1. Preheat oven to 375 degrees.
2. Cut each slice of bread in 3 to 4 strips and set aside.
3. Add the remaining ingredients in a Magic Bullet® or blender. Blend until smooth.
4. Soak the strips of bread in the mixture until completely soaked.
5. Spray a baking sheet with nonstick spray and place saturated sticks on pan.
6. Bake for 15 to 20 minutes depending on the desired level of crunch. Flip the sticks halfway through baking so they are golden brown on each side.
7. Sprinkle with cinnamon and/or stevia (or any other natural sweetener) or your favorite topping such as powdered sugar, low-sugar syrup, jam, etc.

"I thought of this recipe out of the blue one day just messing around in the kitchen while my husband watched football. My fridge was almost empty and we were having some serious French toast cravings, and this is what I came up with! I think the Ezekiel bread really adds some heartiness and flavor to it."

Nutritional Value
Nutritional information is based on 1 serving.

Calories: 195   Fat: 1g   Carbohydrates: 30g   Protein: 13g   Sugar: 5g

breakfast biscuits

Makes 24 mini biscuits.

INGREDIENTS

- 5 egg whites
- 1 egg
- ¼ c. low-fat buttermilk
- ½ c. fat-free cottage cheese
- 1 c. low-fat, shredded sharp cheddar cheese
- 6 oz. (11 slices) turkey bacon, diced
- ½ c. diced sweet onion
- 1 c. Busy Girl Healthy Life™
      Whole-Wheat Bread Crumbs, *pg. 97*
- ½ tsp. olive oil
- ¾ tsp. garlic powder
- ¼ tsp. red pepper flakes
     dash of nutmeg

INSTRUCTIONS

1. Preheat oven to 375 degrees.
2. Heat olive oil in frying pan. Add diced turkey bacon and cook on medium-high until almost crisp.
3. Add diced onions and sauté until onions are opaque. Let cool.
4. Beat egg whites, egg, buttermilk, garlic powder, red pepper flakes and nutmeg in a large mixing bowl.
5. Add cheddar cheese, cottage cheese, turkey bacon, onion and bread crumbs to egg mixture. Salt and pepper to taste, and mix all ingredients well.
6. Spray mini muffin pan with olive oil spray. Fill muffin cups to top, sprinkle lightly with paprika.
7. Bake for 12 to 15 minutes. Remove muffins from pan and let stand for 10 minutes.

> *"This is definitely a great grab-and-go meal! I love to keep them in the freezer and warm them up when I am in the mood for a warm breakfast in a hurry."*

Nutritional Value
Nutritional information is based on 1 biscuit.

Calories: 46   Fat: 1.7g   Carbohydrates: 2.9g   Protein: 5.2g   Sugar: <1g

banana bread

Makes 8 large slices.

INGREDIENTS

1½ c. whole-wheat pastry flour
 2 tsp. baking powder
 ½ tsp. salt
12 packets stevia or ½ c. sugar
 2 Tbsp. sugar-free cocoa powder
 1 egg plus 2 egg whites
 1 c. mashed ripe bananas
 ¾ c. sugar-free applesauce
 1 tsp. vanilla extract

INSTRUCTIONS

1. Preheat oven to 350 degrees.
2. In large mixing bowl, combine all dry ingredients.
   In medium mixing bowl combine all wet ingredients and mix
   well. Add wet mixture to dry mixture and stir until just blended.
3. Spoon batter into a large loaf pan (9" x 5") coated with nonstick spray.
4. Bake for 45 to 50 minutes until knife inserted in middle comes out clean.

"Some of my favorite memories are coming home from school and having the house smell like my mom's banana bread. There is something so comforting about having a slice of this old-fashioned favorite. If I'm really in the mood to get crazy and have a healthy indulgence, I throw a few dark chocolate chips on top!"

Nutritional Value
Nutritional information is based on 1 biscuit.

Calories: 125   Fat: 1g   Carbohydrates: 21.7g   Protein: 4.6g   Sugar: 5.6g

buttermilk sausage gravy & biscuits

Makes 8 servings.

INGREDIENTS

1¼ c. Busy Girl Healthy Life™ Italian Turkey Sausage, *pg. 71*
  3 Tbsp. whole-wheat flour
1½ c. low-sodium chicken stock
1½ c. low-fat buttermilk
     dash of ground nutmeg
  8 whole-grain, light English muffins (split and lightly toasted)
     salt and pepper to taste

INSTRUCTIONS

1. Heat up the sausage in a nonstick cooking pan.
2. Add flour and heat for 1 to 2 minutes more.
3. Add chicken stock, buttermilk and nutmeg, and bring to a soft simmer on medium-high heat stirring constantly until mixture thickens (about 5 minutes).
4. Put ¼ cup of sausage gravy on each half of English muffin. Serve immediately.

Nutritional Value
Nutritional information is based on 1 biscuit.

Calories: 167   Fat: 3.3g   Carbohydrates: 20.6g   Protein: 12.1g   Sugar: 3.6g

pick your patty – breakfast sandwich

Makes 4 egg patties and 18 sausage patties.

INGREDIENTS

Sausage Patty

2	lbs. ground turkey
1	c. oatmeal
3	egg whites
1½	tsp. red pepper flakes
2	tsp. Italian seasoning
2½	tsp. fennel seed
1	tsp. cayenne pepper
1	tsp. garlic powder
3	packets stevia or 2 Tbsp. sugar

Thoroughly mix all ingredients. Make 18 (¾-inch) patties. Fry in a
nonstick frying pan until cooked through. Makes 18 turkey sausage patties.

Egg and Cheese Patty

6	egg whites
1	Tbsp. skim milk
¼	c. reduced-fat shredded sharp cheddar cheese
	pinch of dried thyme leaves
	dash of hot sauce

Beat all ingredients together. Pour in sprayed frying pan and cook until
eggs are set, flipping half way through. Divide into 4 pieces. Makes 4 egg patties.

INSTRUCTIONS

1. Toast whole-grain English muffin. Add one sausage patty and one egg cheese
   patty between muffin for a delicious, healthy and filling breakfast sandwich
   for under 300 calories.

Nutritional Value

1 Sausage Patty
Calories: 93   Fat: 3.9g   Carbohydrates: 2g   Protein: 10.5g   Sugar: 0g

1 Egg and Cheese Patty
Calories: 51   Fat: 1.6g   Carbohydrates: .7g   Protein: 8.3g   Sugar: .7g

sausage egg & cheese breakfast sandwich

Makes 10 sandwiches.

INGREDIENTS

- 1 lb. ground turkey (93/7)
- 2 tsp. olive oil
- ½ tsp. each of garlic powder, red pepper flakes and paprika
- 1 tsp. each Italian seasoning and dried fennel seed
- ¼ tsp. cayenne pepper
  salt and pepper to taste
- 2 eggs
- 8 egg whites
- 10 low-fat cheese slices
- 10 light, whole-grain English muffins (split and lightly toasted)

INSTRUCTIONS

1. Preheat oven to 350 degrees.
2. Beat eggs and egg whites together and pour into a pre-sprayed 9x11 baking dish. Bake in oven for 12 minutes or until eggs are set and cooked through. Cut cooked eggs into 10 pieces.
3. Add all spices to ground turkey and mix well with hands until spices are evenly distributed.
4. Divide turkey into 10 pieces and make them into thin patties. Fry sausage patties in a nonstick frying pan until patties are cooked thoroughly.
5. Put 1 sausage patty, 1 egg patty and 1 slice of cheese on a lightly toasted English muffin and enjoy! It tastes great with a little dijon mustard on the sandwich.

tip:
Freezes well. Make all 10 sandwiches and freeze. To reheat, just wrap frozen sandwich in paper towel and microwave on high for to 1½ minutes.

Nutritional Value
Nutritional information is based on 1 sandwich.

Calories: 245.6   Fat: 8g   Carbohydrates: 20.2g   Protein: 21.2g   Sugar: 2g

mango cream muffins

Makes 12 muffins.

INGREDIENTS

1¼   c. whole-wheat pastry flour
⅔   c. oat flour
1½   tsp. baking powder
½   tsp. baking soda
¼   tsp. salt
1   c. fat-free sour cream or fat-free Greek yogurt
3   Tbsp. light butter, melted
1   tsp. vanilla
2   egg whites, beaten
½   c. low-fat buttermilk
2   c. diced frozen mangos, thawed
12   packets stevia or ½ c. sugar

INSTRUCTIONS

1. Preheat oven to 400 degrees.
2. Mix all dry ingredients together in a mixing bowl.
3. Then in a separate bowl, mix all wet ingredients together.
4. Combine wet and dry ingredients and stir until mostly smooth, some small lumps are ok.
5. Spray muffin pan (12 count) with cooking spray. Fill muffin cups almost totop and bake for 25 minutes or until cooked through.
6. Try the tooth pick trick! Insert toothpick. If it comes out clean, muffins are done.

> "A healthy life is all about balance, and I believe you should be able to eat dessert a few times a week using portion control. Small servings of the healthier options keep this busy girl sane!"

Nutritional Value
Nutritional information is based on 1 muffin.

Calories: 132   Fat: 2.3g   Carbohydrates: 23g   Protein: 8g   Sugar: 5g

breakfast burrito

Makes 8 burritos.

INGREDIENTS

- 10 egg whites
- 2 eggs
- ¼ c. skim milk
- ¼ tsp. ground cumin
- ½ c. diced red pepper
- ½ c. diced green pepper
- ¾ c. diced onion
- 1 finely diced garlic clove
- ¾ c. fat-free cottage cheese
- 1 c. cooked turkey sausage
- ½ c. black beans, drained and rinsed (optional)
  salt and pepper to taste
- 8 whole-wheat 6-inch tortilla shells

INSTRUCTIONS

1. Beat together egg whites, eggs, skim milk and cumin.
2. Mix in cottage cheese, salt and pepper to taste.
3. Sauté onions and peppers until onions are opaque.
4. Add garlic and cook for one minute more.
5. Remove from pan, add egg mixture to pan and scramble eggs on medium-low heat until almost set.
6. Add peppers and onions to egg mixture.
7. Add cooked turkey sausage and black beans, and mix together.
8. Put ½ c. of egg mixture into a warm whole-wheat tortilla shell, garnish with diced fresh tomatoes and roll into burrito. May garnish with 1 Tbsp. of your favorite salsa for extra spice.

Store cooked egg mixture in the refrigerator. For a quick breakfast on the go, just put ½ c. of filling in tortilla shell, garnish with fresh diced tomato and microwave for one minute.

Nutritional Value

Nutritional information is based on ½ c. egg serving with 1 whole-wheat tortilla shell.

Calories: 144   Fat: 4.7g   Carbohydrates: 15g   Protein: 20g   Sugar: 1.5g

spinach artichoke frittata

Makes 4 generous servings.

INGREDIENTS

- 8 oz. frozen chopped spinach, thawed and water squeezed out
- 9 oz. jar marinated artichoke hearts, drained and chopped
- ¾ to 1 c. chopped sweet onions
  pinch of red pepper flakes
- ½ c. fat-free cottage cheese
- 3 wedges Laughing Cow® Light Swiss Cheese
- 8 egg whites
- 2 eggs
- ¼ tsp. garlic powder
  splash of water
  pinch of nutmeg

INSTRUCTIONS

1. Preheat oven to 350 degrees.
2. Generously spray frying pan with cooking spray. Sauté spinach, onion, artichoke and red pepper flakes until onion is tender. Add cottage cheese, Laughing Cow and cook until cheese melts.
3. Beat egg whites, eggs and garlic powder with a splash of water.
4. Add to spinach and cheese mixture. Cook for 2 minutes.
5. Place the mixture into a 10- to 12-inch baking dish. Sprinkle top with a pinch of nutmeg and bake for 20 minutes or until frittata is set. Remove from oven and let stand for 5 to 10 minutes.

Leftovers are great reheated!

Nutritional Value

Nutritional information is based on about ¼ of dish.

Calories: 196   Fat: 7.8g   Carbohydrates: 11.8g   Protein: 17.5g   Sugar: 3.9g

broccoli mushroom onion frittata

Makes 4 generous servings.

INGREDIENTS

1½ c. chopped broccoli
 1 4oz. can mushrooms,
    drained and diced
 ¾ to 1c. diced sweet onion
 ½ c. fat-free cottage cheese
 3 wedges Laughing Cow®
    Light Swiss Cheese
 8 egg whites
 2 eggs
    splash of water
 ½ tsp. garlic powder
    pinch of red pepper flakes
 ⅛ tsp. dried thyme leaves

INSTRUCTIONS

1. Preheat oven to 350 degrees.
2. Generously spray frying pan with cooking spray. Sauté broccoli, mushrooms, onion and red pepper flakes until tender. Add cottage cheese, Laughing Cow and cook until cheese melts.
3. Beat egg whites, eggs and garlic powder with a splash of water.
4. Add to broccoli and cheese mixture. Cook for 2 minutes.
5. Place the mixture into a 10- to 12-inch baking dish. Bake for 20 minutes or until frittata is set. Remove from oven and let stand for 5 to 10 minutes.

Leftovers are great reheated!

Nutritional Value

Nutritional information is based on about ¼ of dish.

Calories: 153.5   Fat: 3.4g   Carbohydrates: 7.8g   Protein: 17.6g   Sugar: 4.5g

appetizers

sausage mushroom tartlets

Makes 15 tartlets.

INGREDIENTS

1½ c. finely diced portobello mushrooms
¼ c. each of finely diced celery and water chestnuts
2 Tbsp. finely diced onion
½ c. Busy Girl Healthy Life™ Italian Turkey Sausage, *pg. 71*
3 oz. fat-free cream cheese, room temperature
1 box (15 count) mini phyllo cups
   salt and pepper to taste

INSTRUCTIONS

1. Preheat oven to 375 degrees.
2. Put finely diced mushroom, celery, water chestnuts and onion
   in microwave-safe bowl. Microwave on high for one minute.
3. Add cream cheese and sausage to hot mixture.
   Mix well until cream cheese is melted.
4. Fill mini phyllo cups with mixture.
5. Bake in oven for 12 to 15 minutes.

Nutritional Value
Nutritional information is based on 1 tartlet.

Calories: 32   Fat: .9g   Carbohydrates: 3.5g   Protein: 2.7g   Sugar: <1g

bacon, tomato and chive deviled eggs

Makes 12 deviled eggs.

INGREDIENTS

  6 hard-boiled eggs (discard 3 of the yolks)
  3 Tbsp. fat-free Greek yogurt
  1 Tbsp. low-fat mayo
  1 tsp. dijon mustard
  1 packet stevia or 2 tsp. sugar
  1 Tbsp. finely chopped chives
     paprika
  ¼ tsp. onion powder
  ¼ tsp. garlic powder
  ⅛ tsp. red pepper flakes
  3 Tbsp. finely chopped tomatoes (optional)
  3 Tbsp. finely chopped
  4 to 5 strips cooked turkey bacon

INSTRUCTIONS

1. Cut eggs in half lengthwise.
2. Discard three of the yolks; put the other three yolks in a bowl with the yogurt, mayo, mustard and sweetener.
3. Mash yolks and mix ingredients well.
4. Add the onion powder, garlic powder and red pepper flakes. Mix well.
5. Stir in the tomatoes and bacon, salt and pepper to taste.
6. Fill the egg whites with the mixture. Lightly sprinkle with paprika and top the eggs with the chives.
7. Chill for about an hour.

tip:

For the perfect hard-boiled egg, cover eggs with cold water and heat on high uncovered until water comes to a rolling boil. Take eggs off the heat and let sit covered for 20 minutes. Then, drain eggs and put in cold water until cooled. Eggs peel easily and no more dark color around the yolk!

Nutritional Value
Nutritional information based on 1 deviled egg.

Calories: 32   Fat: 4g   Carbohydrates: <1g   Protein: 1.6g   Sugar: <1g

crab tartlets

Makes 15 tartlets.

INGREDIENTS

- ⅓ c. each finely diced celery and sweet red pepper
- 2 Tbsp. finely diced onion
- 4 oz. iced imitation crab
  (can use real crab or shrimp)
- ¼ tsp. garlic powder
- 3 oz. fat-free cream cheese, room temperature
- 1 Tbsp. low-fat mayo or fat-free Greek yogurt
- 1 box (15 count) mini phyllo cups
  salt and pepper to taste

INSTRUCTIONS

1. Preheat oven to 375 degrees.
2. Put finely diced pepper, celery and onion in microwave-safe bowl. Microwave on high for 1 minute.
3. Add cream cheese, mayo, garlic powder and crab to hot mixture. Mix well until cream cheese is melted.
4. Fill mini phyllo cups with mixture.
5. Bake in oven for 12 to 15 minutes.

Nutritional Value
Nutritional information based on 1 tartlet.

Calories: 29   Fat: .7g   Carbohydrates: 4g   Protein: 2g   Sugar: <1g

hot banana pepper goat cheese boats

Makes 16 boats.

INGREDIENTS

8   banana peppers (about 4 inches long each)
8   tsp. goat cheese

INSTRUCTIONS

1. Preheat oven to 450 degrees.
2. Slice peppers in half lengthwise. Remove seeds.
3. Bake in hot oven for 3 to 4 minutes until peppers are cooked, but still firm.
4. Remove from oven and let cool.
5. Spread ½ tsp. of goat cheese on each pepper half.

Nutritional Value
Nutritional information based on 1 boat.

Calories: 7.5   Fat: .4g   Carbohydrates: <1g   Protein: <1g   Sugar: 0g

asian meatballs

Makes 40 meatballs.

INGREDIENTS

1½ lbs. ground turkey (93/7)
 2 c. finely diced sweet onion
 1 c. finely diced celery
 2 c. finely shredded cabbage
1½ Tbsp. finely minced fresh ginger
 ¼ c. finely minced jalapeño,
     seeds and ribs removed
 2 egg whites
 ½ c. Busy Girl Healthy Life™
     Whole-Wheat Bread Crumbs, *pg. 97*
 ¼ c. low-sodium soy sauce
 2 tsp. toasted sesame oil
 2 Tbsp. sweet Asian chili sauce
 3 packets stevia or 2 Tbsp. sugar
     salt and pepper to taste

INSTRUCTIONS

1. Preheat oven to 375 degrees.
2. Combine all ingredients and mix thoroughly.
3. Roll mixture into 40 quarter-size meatballs.
4. Put meatballs on a nonstick baking sheet sprayed with nonstick cooking spray.
5. Bake in oven for 25 to 30 minutes, or until meatballs are thoroughly cooked.

"If you're going to make meatballs, make sure it's these! Bring these to your parties or throw in the freezer to eat or add to any dish. These are definitely a crowd pleaser, so don't plan on any leftovers!"

Nutritional Value
Nutritional information based on 1 meatball.

Calories: 38.4   Fat: 1.4g   Carbohydrates: 1.4g   Protein: 3.7g   Sugar: <1g

pizza tartlets

Makes 15 tartlets.

INGREDIENTS

⅓ c. finely diced mushrooms
and red bell pepper
2 Tbsp. finely diced onion
2-3 Tbsp. pizza sauce
¼ c. Busy Girl Healthy Life™
Italian Turkey Sausage, *pg. 71*
¼ c. finely diced turkey pepperoni
¼ c. shredded, low-fat mozzarella cheese
1 box (15 count) mini phyllo cups
salt and pepper to taste

INSTRUCTIONS

1. Preheat oven to 375 degrees.
2. Put finely diced mushroom, onion
and pepper in microwave safe bowl.
Microwave on high for 1 minute.
3. Add rest of ingredients and mix well.
4. Fill mini phyllo cups with mixture.
5. Bake in oven for 12 to 15 minutes.

"Cute, impressive and heavenly. These little mini bites of pizza are aways a hit. They pack so much flavor and are just what the doctor ordered when the mood for a big slice arises! Who doesn't like a party where there's pizza?"

Nutritional Value
Nutritional information based on 1 tartlet.

| Calories: 28.9 | Fat: 1.3g | Carbohydrates: 2.6g | Protein: 2.3g | Sugar: <1g |

stuffed mushrooms

Makes 20 to 24 stuffed mushrooms
(depending on mushroom size).

INGREDIENTS

- 16 oz. fresh portabella mushrooms
- ¾ c. Busy Girl Healthy Life™
  Italian Turkey Sausage, *pg. 71*
- 2 Tbsp. dried bread crumbs
- 1 packet stevia or 2 tsp. sugar (optional)
- ½ c. finely chopped onion
- ½ c. finely chopped celery
- 1 c. shredded, low-fat
  mozzarella cheese
- 2 Tbsp. grated Parmesan
  finely chopped mushroom stems,
  (removed from mushrooms)
- 1 egg white
  salt and pepper to taste

INSTRUCTIONS

1. Preheat oven to 375 degrees.
2. Remove stems from mushroom caps and finely chop the stems.
3. Sauté onions, celery and chopped stems until tender. Cool.
4. Combine onion mixture, sausage, cheese, egg white and bread crumbs, and mix well.
5. Stuff the mushrooms with mixture.
6. Bake for about 15 to 20 minutes or until golden.

*"These are one of the most popular Busy Girl Healthy Life™
recipes. Easy to make, take and pop in your mouth!"*

Nutritional Value
Nutritional information based on 1 stuffed mushroom.

Calories: 29   Fat: 1.5g   Carbohydrates: 1.4g   Protein: 3.6g   Sugar: <1g

salads, dressings & soups

veggie potato salad

Makes 12 servings.

INGREDIENTS

Salad

- 5 medium red potatoes
- 5 c. cauliflower florets
- ⅔ c. diced radishes
- 1 c. diced English cucumber
- ½ c. diced red onion
- 1 c. diced celery
- 6 hard-boiled egg whites, diced

Dressing

- 6 oz. fat-free Greek yogurt
- ½ c. low-fat mayo
- 1 Tbsp. dijon mustard
- ¾ c. low-fat buttermilk
- ½ tsp. dried tarragon leaves
- ½ tsp. garlic powder
- 1 Tbsp. light olive oil
- 2 packets stevia or 4 tsp. sugar

INSTRUCTIONS

1. Boil potatoes, drain and cool. Dice potatoes into ½-inch cubes.
2. Steam cauliflower until tender, dice cauliflower.
3. Mix all salad ingredients together.
4. In separate bowl, combine all dressing ingredients and whisk together until thoroughly mixed.
5. Add dressing to salad ingredients and mix well.
6. Let sit in refrigerator for at least 1 hour before serving.

"You never have go to a picnic empty handed when you have this tasty recipe! The best part is knowing you have something healthy to eat while you're there!"

Nutritional Value
Nutritional information is based on 1 cup of salad.

Calories: 131   Fat: 2.4g   Carbohydrates: 18.7g   Protein: 6.6g   Sugar: 3.5g

bean and veggie salad

Makes 6 servings.

INGREDIENTS

¾ c. each canned black beans, chick peas and great northern beans (drained and rinsed)
½ c. diced red onion
1 c. (heaping) diced fresh tomatoes
1 c. each diced English cucumbers, red bell pepper and celery
2 to 3 oz. crumbled goat cheese
   salt and pepper to taste
   Balsamic Dressing, *pg. 34*

INSTRUCTIONS

1. Combine all ingredients, and mix well.
2. Dress with balsamic dressing.

"One of the most amazing things about eating healthy is you actually start craving vegetables! I never thought it would happen to me. This salad is so fresh and satisfying, and the goat cheese is the perfect complement to this dish!"

Nutritional Value
Nutritional information is based on 1 cup of salad. Dressing not included, see *pg. 34*.

Calories: 46 ❁ Fat: 1.7g ❁ Carbohydrates: 2.9g ❁ Protein: 5.2g ❁ Sugar: <1g

greek orzo salad

Makes about 4 servings.

INGREDIENTS

⅔ c. whole-wheat orzo, uncooked
2 c. fresh tomatoes, diced
1 c. English cucumber, diced
1 small diced red onion
1 diced green bell pepper
½ c. diced black or kalamata olives
3 oz. crumbled fat-free feta cheese
½ c. Busy Girl Healthy Life™ Greek Dressing, *pg. 36*

INSTRUCTIONS

1. Cook orzo according to directions on package. Drain and cool.
2. Mix all ingredients together.
3. Add dressing and mix well.

"Even your yia yia would approve of this one! Healthy and mouth watering!"

Nutritional Value
Nutritional information is based on ¼ of salad.

Calories: 202 Fat: 5g Carbohydrates: 22g Protein: 10g Sugar: 4g

salad niçoise

Makes 4 heaping servings.

INGREDIENTS

- 1 c. blanched green beans
- 2 medium red potatoes, cooked and chopped
- ⅓ c. diced red onion
- ½ c. black or kalamata olives
- 3 hard-boiled egg whites, chopped
- ¾ c. diced red bell pepper
- 1 c. diced fresh tomato
- 2 5 oz. cans solid white tuna, drained and chopped
- 4 c. chopped romaine lettuce
  Busy Girl Healthy Life™
  Greek Dressing, *pg. 36*

INSTRUCTIONS

1. Blanch green beans for two minutes in boiling water until bright green.
2. Drain and rinse in cold water to stop cooking process.
3. Cook potatoes and let cool. Chopped into half-inch cubes.
4. Combine all salad ingredients and mix well.
5. Add ½ c. Greek dressing and mix well. Serve immediately.

Nutritional Value

Nutritional information is based on ¼ of salad.

Calories: 215.2   Fat: 4.6g   Carbohydrates: 18.3g   Protein: 19g   Sugar: 5g

shrimp salad with avocado dressing

Makes about 4 servings.

INGREDIENTS

- 1 lb. peeled, deveined, cooked shrimp, chopped
- ⅔ c. diced sweet red bell pepper
- ⅔ c. diced sweet green bell pepper
- 1 c. diced celery
- ¼ c. finely diced red onion
  salt and pepper to taste
- ½ c. Busy Girl Healthy Life™ Avocado Dressing, *pg. 33*

INSTRUCTIONS

1. Combine shrimp and veggies and mix well. Salt and pepper to taste.
2. Stir in dressing.
3. Serve on a bed of chopped lettuce.

Nutritional Value

Nutritional information is based on ¼ of salad.

Calories: 144.6   Fat: 2.3g   Carbohydrates: 5.4g   Protein: 22.5g   Sugar: 2.2g

smoked salmon pasta salad

Makes 6 servings.

INGREDIENTS

6 oz. whole-wheat macaroni
6 oz. smoked salmon, chopped
¼ c. diced red onion
1 c. diced red bell pepper
1 c. frozen baby peas, thawed
1 c. diced English cucumber
1 c. packed fresh baby spinach
   salt and pepper to taste
¾ c. Busy Girl Healthy Life™
   Buttermilk Dill Dressing, *pg. 38*

INSTRUCTIONS

1. Cook macaroni according to directions. Drain and cool.
2. Mix macaroni, salmon and veggies together.
3. Add buttermilk dressing and mix well.
4. Let marinate in refrigerator for 1 hour before serving.

Nutritional Value

Nutritional information is based on ⅙ of salad.

Calories: 220   Fat: 6.3g   Carbohydrates: 22g   Protein: 13g   Sugar: 4.4g

strawberry feta spinach salad

Makes about 4 servings.

INGREDIENTS

   5 c. packed fresh baby spinach
   ¾ c. diced fresh tomato
   ⅓ c. diced red onion
   ¾ c. sliced strawberries
   ½ c. mandarin oranges packed
       in water, drained
   1 c. diced English cucumber
   ⅓ c. sliced water chestnuts
   ⅓ c. crumbled fat-free feta cheese
   ½ c. Busy Girl Healthy Life™
       Oriental Dressing, *pg. 35*

INSTRUCTIONS

1. Mix all ingredients together.
2. Pour ½ cup Oriental Dressing
   over salad and mix well.
3. Serve immediately. Can add grilled
   chicken to make a main-course salad
   packed with protein.

Nutritional Value

Nutritional information is based on ¼ of salad.

Calories: 142   Fat: 3.8g   Carbohydrates: 14.8g   Protein: 10g   Sugar: 7.1g

asparagus walnut salad

Makes 4 heaping servings.

INGREDIENTS

  2 c. chopped fresh asparagus
     (chopped to pea size)
½ c. chopped sweet onion
¾ c. grated Parmesan cheese
½ c. diced turkey bacon (4-5 cooked slices)
½ c. roasted walnuts, chopped
     drizzle of red wine or balsamic vinegar
     drizzle of your favorite olive oil
     salt and pepper to taste

INSTRUCTIONS

1. Cut lower half of asparagus off, and toss or freeze for asparagus soup.
2. Chop upper half of asparagus into pea-size pieces.
3. Add all other ingredients to chopped asparagus and mix well.
4. Drizzle with your favorite vinegar and olive oil. Salt and pepper to taste.
5. Chill for 1 to 2 hours.

Don't panic about the fat content, it's good fat (omega 3) from the walnuts.

hint:

Can substitute chicken, turkey or crab in place of the bacon. Just put a cup of the asparagus salad on top of your favorite lettuce, and enjoy.

Nutritional Value

Nutritional information is based on ¼ of salad.

Calories: 236   Fat: 16g   Carbohydrates: 8g   Protein: 14g   Sugar: 3g

japanese steak salad with peanut dressing

Makes about 4 servings.

INGREDIENTS

- 12 oz. beef tenderloin (grilled medium rare, sliced thinly into strips)
- 1 c. pea pods, blanched
- 2 small carrots, julienned
- 1 small diced red bell pepper
- ¼ c. diced red onion
- 1 c. diced celery
- 1 c. fresh baby bella mushrooms, sliced
- 6 c. chopped romaine lettuce
  Busy Girl Healthy Life™
  Peanut Dressing, *pg. 32*

INSTRUCTIONS

1. Mix all ingredients together.
2. Pour ½ cup peanut dressing over salad and mix well.
3. Serve immediately.

Nutritional Value

Nutritional information is based on ¼ of salad.

Calories: 239 ☀ Fat: 8.5g ☀ Carbohydrates: 6.7g ☀ Protein: 22.1g ☀ Sugar: 8.2g

chicken caesar salad

Makes 4 heaping servings.

INGREDIENTS

4   4 oz. grilled boneless,
    skinless chicken breasts
6   c. diced romaine lettuce
1   small red onion, sliced very thin
4   hard-boiled egg whites, chopped
1   c. Busy Girl Healthy Life™
    Whole-Wheat Croutons, *pg. 99*
2   Tbsp. grated Parmesan cheese
    Salt and pepper to taste
½   c. Busy Girl Healthy Life™
    Caesar Dressing, *pg. 37*

INSTRUCTIONS

1. Slice grilled chicken in thin strips.
2. Mix all other ingredients together.
3. Top with ¼ of chicken strips.
4. Drizzle with Caesar dressing.

"I am a salad junkie and I know a good Caesar when I see one. I could seriously eat salad every day and be happy! My husband and I like to rate all of our Caesar salads whenever we're traveling. This recipe is still one of the best!"

Nutritional Value

Nutritional information is based on ¼ of salad.

Calories: 243.5   Fat: 7.4g   Carbohydrates: 7.2g   Protein: 34.3g   Sugar: 3.2g

asian coleslaw

Makes about 9 cups.

INGREDIENTS

Dressing
¼ c. toasted sesame oil
¼ c. white wine or rice wine vinegar
¼ c. low-sodium chicken broth
2 Tbsp. low-sodium soy sauce
5 packets stevia or 3 Tbsp. sugar
¼ to ½ tsp. red pepper flakes

Coleslaw
2 Tbsp. light butter
¼ c. sliced or slivered almonds
1 Tbsp. sesame seeds
2 oz. Chinese noodles misna
   (in Oriental foods aisle)
1 16 oz. bag coleslaw cabbage mix
1 c. diced celery
1 c. diced snap peas
¾ c. diced green onion
1 8 oz. can diced water chestnuts

INSTRUCTIONS

Dressing:
1. Combine dressing ingredients in covered jar and shake well.

Coleslaw:
2. Melt butter in skillet. Brown noodles, almonds and sesame seeds.
    Remove noodle mixture onto a paper towel to cool.
3. Toss cabbage, celery, snap peas, green onion, water chestnuts and noodle
    mixture in large bowl. Add dressing and toss well. Salt and pepper to taste.
4. Let stand for 20 minutes before serving.

*"To serve as an entree, add 4 oz. cooked chicken to coleslaw.
I love to use chopsticks to savor every little bite!"*

Nutritional Value
Nutritional information is based on 1 cup.
Calories: 140   Fat: 8.5g   Carbohydrates: 9.3g   Protein: 3g   Sugar: 2.2g

japanese peanut dressing

Makes ¾ cup.

INGREDIENTS

2 Tbsp. natural peanut butter or PB2
2 Tbsp. lemon juice
2 Tbsp. soy sauce
3 Tbsp. sugar-free or natural maple syrup
1½ tsp. sesame oil
¼ tsp. garlic powder
¼ tsp. ground ginger
¼ c. chicken stock
salt and pepper to taste

INSTRUCTIONS

1. Mix all ingredients together in blender on medium speed until well blended.

Nutritional Value
Nutritional information is based on 1 Tbsp.

Calories: 23.6   Fat: 1.6g   Carbohydrates: 1.8g   Protein: <1g   Sugar: <1g

avocado dressing

Makes about 1½ cups.

INGREDIENTS

- 1   avocado
- ¼   c. low-fat buttermilk
- 5   oz. fat-free dressing
- ¼   c. chicken stock
- ¼   c. lime juice
- 1   tsp. chili powder
- ¼   tsp. each garlic powder and onion powder
- 1   packet stevia or 2 tsp. sugar

INSTRUCTIONS

1. Remove pit from avocado. Scoop avocado out of shell. Put avocado and remaining ingredients in blender. Blend on high speed until creamy.
2. Store in glass container. Put plastic wrap on top of dressing in container so dressing is not exposed to air. Put cover on container and store in the refrigerator.

** If desired, recipe can easily be divided in half.**

Nutritional Value
Nutritional information is based on 1 Tbsp.

Calories: 14.8   Fat: .9g   Carbohydrates: .8g   Protein: .9g   Sugar: .5g

balsamic dressing

Makes ½ cup.

INGREDIENTS

- 2 Tbsp. balsamic vinegar
- 1½ Tbsp. lemon juice
- 1 Tbsp. light olive oil
- ⅓ c. low-sodium chicken stock
- ¼ tsp. garlic powder
- 1 packet stevia or 2 tsp. sugar
  salt and pepper to taste

INSTRUCTIONS

1. Mix all ingredients together in blender on low speed until well blended.

Nutritional Value
Nutritional information is based on 1 Tbsp.

Calories: 17.4   Fat: 1.8g   Carbohydrates: <1g   Protein: 0g   Sugar: <1g

oriental dressing

Makes ¾ cup.

INGREDIENTS

5 tsp. rice wine vinegar
4 tsp. soy sauce
1 Tbsp. lemon juice
1 tsp. sesame seeds
1 tsp. dijon mustard
1 Tbsp. light olive oil
1½ tsp. sesame oil
¼ c. low-sodium chicken stock
2 packets stevia or 1½ Tbsp. sugar

INSTRUCTIONS

1. Mix all ingredients together in blender on low speed until well blended.

Nutritional Value
Nutritional information is based on 1 Tbsp.

Calories: 18.5   Fat: 1.8g   Carbohydrates: <1g   Protein: <1g   Sugar: <1g

greek dressing

Makes ¾ cup.

INGREDIENTS

2 Tbsp. lemon juice
2 Tbsp. red wine vinegar
¼ tsp. garlic powder
1 tsp. dried oregano
1½ Tbsp. light olive oil
¼ c. chicken stock
1 packet stevia or 2 tsp. sugar

INSTRUCTIONS

1. Mix all ingredients together in blender on low speed until well blended.

Nutritional Value
Nutritional information is based on 1 Tbsp.

Calories: 16.6   Fat: 1.8g   Carbohydrates: <1g   Protein: 0g   Sugar: <1g

caesar salad dressing

Makes ⅔ cup.

INGREDIENTS

1	hard-boiled egg yolk
4	tsp. lemon juice
1	Tbsp. red wine vinegar
¼	tsp. garlic powder
1	Tbsp. light olive oil
1½	tsp. dijon mustard
1	Tbsp. grated Parmesan
¼	c. chicken stock

INSTRUCTIONS

1. Mash egg yolk with a fork.
2. Add yolk and Parmesan to chicken stock and heat on stove, stirring until yolk is dissolved. Cool stock.
3. Mix all ingredients in blender on medium speed until well blended. Salt and pepper to taste.

Nutritional Value
Nutritional information is based on 1 Tbsp.

Calories: 19.5   Fat: 1.8g   Carbohydrates: <1g   Protein: 5g   Sugar: <1g

buttermilk dill dressing

Makes 1 cup.

INGREDIENTS

- ½ c. + 2 Tbsp. low-fat buttermilk
- ¼ c. fat-free Greek yogurt
- 2 Tbsp. low-fat mayo
- 2 Tbsp. lemon juice
- 1 Tbsp. olive oil
- 1½ tsp. dried dill weed
- ¼ tsp. garlic powder
- 1 packet stevia or 2 tsp. sugar

INSTRUCTIONS

1. Thoroughly mix all ingredients. Store in glass container and keep refrigerated.

Nutritional Value
Nutritional information is based on 1 Tbsp.

Calories: 16 ⬤ Fat: 1.1g ⬤ Carbohydrates: 1g ⬤ Protein: .8g ⬤ Sugar: .8g

italian wedding soup

Makes 15 servings.

INGREDIENTS

2	tsp. olive oil
1	c. diced onion
1	c. diced celery
¾	c. diced red or green sweet pepper
2	Tbsp. minced garlic
2	Tbsp. light butter (or olive oil)
3	Tbsp. flour
½	c. red wine (or beef stock)
1	15 oz. can diced tomatoes
4	c. chicken stock
4	c. beef stock
2	bay leaves
1½	tsp. Italian seasoning
⅛	tsp. red pepper flakes
4	packets stevia or 3 Tbsp. sugar
1	lb. ground turkey sausage
2	c. cooked whole-grain orzo (1 c. uncooked)
10	oz. frozen chopped spinach, thawed and drained
½	c. low-fat buttermilk
⅓	c. grated Parmesan

"When I was little, I was obsessed with soup. My grandma used to take me out for soup all the time. She still tells me stories about how it was the only thing I ever ordered. This soup is perfect for cold winter nights, but also goes perfect with the Busy Girl Healthy Life™ Caesar Salad in the summer. And nothing makes me feel better than some hot soup if I am a little under the weather."

INSTRUCTIONS

1. Sauté celery, onion, sweet pepper and garlic in olive oil until tender (4 to 5 minutes).
2. Stir in butter and flour — cook for 1 minute.
3. Add wine and stir until thickened.
4. Add chicken stock, beef stock and diced tomatoes, and bring to a soft boil.
5. Turn heat down to low and add bay leaves, Italian seasoning and red pepper flakes. Add turkey sausage, cooked orzo and spinach. Stir in buttermilk, sweetener and Parmesan.
6. Simmer for 15 to 20 minutes.

hint:

Soup freezes well. Divide into 1-cup containers and freeze. Just grab a container to take with you to work, microwave, and enjoy a great healthy lunch!

Nutritional Value
Nutritional information is based on 1 cup.

Calories: 130 ● Fat: 4g ● Carbohydrates: 9.2g ● Protein: 10g ● Sugar: 1.8g

pastas & vegetables

italian marinated veggies

Makes 7 servings.

INGREDIENTS

- 1 c. julienne carrots
- 1 c. fresh mushrooms, cut in half
- 1 c. green beans, blanched
- 1 c. broccoli florets
- 1 c. cauliflower florets
- 1 c. radishes (quartered)
- 1 c. celery, cut into two-inch pieces

Marinade:

- ¼ c. balsamic vinegar
- ¼ c. low-sodium chicken stock
- 2 Tbsp. extra virgin olive oil
- ½ tsp. Italian seasoning
- ¼ tsp. garlic powder
- ¼ tsp. onion powder
- 1 packet stevia or 2 tsp. sugar

INSTRUCTIONS

1. In a glass jar with cover, combine all marinade ingredients. Shake well until all ingredients are combined.
2. Pour marinade over veggies and mix well.
3. Let veggies marinate for at least 1 hour before serving.

> "By request, these are at every family gathering we have! I always fill up on these first so I don't go overboard on the other goodies!"

Nutritional Value

Nutritional information is based on 1 cup.

Calories: 68 ❀ Fat: 4g ❀ Carbohydrates: 3.6g ❀ Protein: 1.7g ❀ Sugar: 1.9g

eggplant parmigiana

Makes 8 servings.

INGREDIENTS

1   medium eggplant
2   large egg whites
¼   c. low-fat buttermilk
1   to 1½ c. Busy Girl Healthy Life™
    Whole-Wheat Bread Crumbs, *pg. 97*
½   tsp. Italian seasoning
¾   tsp. each onion powder and
    garlic powder, divided
½   c. low-fat shredded mozzarella cheese
½   c. shredded Parmesan
1   15 oz. can crushed tomatoes
⅛   tsp. each cayenne pepper and
    red pepper flakes
2-3 packets of stevia or 4 tsp. sugar

INSTRUCTIONS

1. Preheat oven to 425 degrees.
2. Whisk together egg whites, buttermilk and ¼ tsp. each of the onion and garlic powder.
3. In separate bowl, mix bread crumbs, ¼ tsp. each onion and garlic powder,
    and Italian seasoning.
4. Peel and slice eggplant into 8 slices lengthwise.
5. Dip eggplant in egg mixture, and then dredge in bread crumbs, patting down to make
    sure eggplant is completely covered.
6. Put eggplant on an 11 x 16 jelly roll pan sprayed with cooking spray.
7. Spray top of eggplant with cooking spray and bake for 20 to 25 minutes. Turn eggplant
    halfway through cooking time.
8. While eggplant is baking, simmer tomatoes, ¼ tsp. each onion and garlic powder, Italian
    seasoning, cayenne pepper, red pepper flakes and sweetener on stove top for 10 minutes.
9. Spread tomato sauce over eggplant, sprinkle with mozzarella and Parmesan cheeses.
10. Return to oven and bake about 5 minutes or until cheese melts.

*"A family favorite for dinner and leftovers! Anything that ends in 'parmigiana'
has to be amazing! Your mouth will be singing 'That's amoré' in no time.
Just remember, chew first and sing later!"*

Nutritional Value
Nutritional information is based on 1 slice eggplant and ⅛ of sauce

Calories: 99.6 ❖ Fat: 2.8g ❖ Carbohydrates: 8.7g ❖ Protein: 8.4g ❖ Sugar: 2.6g

italian green beans

Makes 6 servings.

INGREDIENTS

1   lb. fresh green beans,
    washed and stems removed
1   small red onion, thinly sliced
6   oz. fresh portobello mushrooms, sliced
1   15 oz. can petite diced tomatoes
    with basil, drained
½   tsp. Italian seasoning
¼   tsp. garlic powder
2   Tbsp. grated Parmesan cheese
½   packet stevia or 1 tsp. sugar
    salt and pepper to taste

INSTRUCTIONS

1. Blanche green beans in salted boiling water for 2 minutes.
   Drain and rinse in cold ice water until cooled to stop the cooking process.
2. Spray nonstick frying pan with nonstick spray. Sauté mushrooms and
   onions until caramelized (5 to 8 minutes).
3. Add green beans and sauté until tender crisp.
4. Add tomatoes and seasonings. Cook for another 3 minutes.
5. Remove and place on serving platter and sprinkle with the cheese.

Nutritional Value
Nutritional information is based on ⅙ of platter.

Calories: 66.3   Fat: .5g   Carbohydrates: 7g   Protein: 3.3g   Sugar: 4.5g

mango coconut quinoa

Makes 6 servings.

INGREDIENTS

- ¾ c. quinoa
- 1½ c. coconut milk
- ¼ tsp. each red pepper flakes, garlic powder and cayenne pepper
- 1 small diced red onion
- 1 c. diced red bell pepper
- 1 c. diced English cucumber
- 1 12 oz. bag frozen mangos, thawed and diced
- 2 Tbsp. unsweetened coconut salt and pepper to taste

INSTRUCTIONS

1. Cook quinoa according to package directions, substituting coconut milk in place of the liquid.
2. Add red pepper flakes, garlic powder and cayenne pepper to quinoa before cooking.
3. Add remaining ingredients with cooked quinoa. Mix well. Salt and pepper to taste.

"Add a cabana and I am in heaven! I may live in Minnesota but this dish makes me feel like I'm on a tropical vacation!"

Nutritional Value

Nutritional information is based on ⅙ of dish.

Calories: 156.3 ❀ Fat: 2.4g ❀ Carbohydrates: 26g ❀ Protein: 4g ❀ Sugar: 4.6g

no-sin green bean casserole

Makes 5 cups.

INGREDIENTS

- 2 medium onions, thinly sliced
- 8 oz. sliced mushrooms, fresh or canned
- 2 tsp. extra-virgin olive oil, divided
- 2 16 oz. bags whole green beans, thawed and dried
- 1 can water chestnuts, slivered
- 2 tsp. minced garlic
- 2 Tbsp. flour
- ½ c. white wine
- ½ c. low-fat buttermilk
- ½ c. slivered toasted almonds
- 2 Tbsp. Parmesan cheese
  salt and pepper to taste

INSTRUCTIONS

1. Preheat oven to 350 degrees.
2. In a large frying pan, add 1 tsp. extra-virgin olive oil, onions and mushrooms. Cook on medium-high heat until onions are almost caramelized.
3. Add green beans, water chestnuts, garlic, salt and pepper to taste. Stir fry until beans are tender crisp.
4. Add 1 tsp. extra-virgin olive oil, flour and cook for 1 minute.
5. Stir in wine and mix well.
6. Stir in buttermilk and almonds.
7. Transfer to a baking dish and sprinkle with 2 Tbsp. Parmesan cheese.
8. Bake until heated through and cheese is golden brown (about 15 to 20 minutes).

> *"Just the right blend of wine, Parmesan and creaminess. This recipe makes me think, 'Wow, I'm a good cook!' every time I make this! Ha!"*

tip:

This recipe can be doubled or tripled, packaged in desired serving sizes and frozen.

Nutritional Value

Nutritional information is based on ⅔ cup.

Calories: 121 ❁ Fat: 3g ❁ Carbohydrates: 16g ❁ Protein: 4g ❁ Sugar: 4g

baked mac & cheese

Makes 6 servings as an appetizer.
Makes 4 servings as an entree.

INGREDIENTS

 2   cups whole-wheat elbow noodles
 ¼   c. whole-wheat flour
 2   Tbsp. sea salt
     (and pepper if desired) to taste
 1   c. skim milk
 4   oz. low-fat shredded Swiss cheese
 4   oz. low-fat shredded cheddar cheese

INSTRUCTIONS

1. Preheat oven to 375 degrees.
2. Boil noodles on stove top
   according to package directions.
3. Drain noodles and transfer to casserole dish. Slowly add whole-wheat
   flour and milk while stirring. Add salt and cheese. Mix well.
4. Sprinkle top with bread crumbs.
5. Bake in oven until top is lightly brown
   (about 15 to 20 minutes).

Optional

1. ⅛ c. Busy Girl Healthy Life™ Whole-Wheat Bread Crumbs, (*pg. 97*) and 2 Tbsp. Parmesan
   cheese may be sprinkled on top before baking to add a crispy baked layer over the top.

2. You may add more or less cheese to this recipe depending on what you prefer!
   It does not affect how it cooks or turns out! Feel free to add some veggies or Busy Girl
   Italian Turkey Sausage (*pg. 71*) for a complete dinner for the family!

> *"This is a recipe from my dear friend, Kristi Youngdahl. We made this together for an episode of Busy Girl. This is 100% kid tested and mother approved! The big kids sure like it, too!"*

Nutritional Value

Nutritional information is based on ⅙ or ¼ serving.

Appetizer
Calories: 193.3   ◎   Fat: 2.7g   ◎   Carbohydrates: 25g   ◎   Protein: 9.2g   ◎   Sugar: 3.5g

Entree
Calories: 290   ◎   Fat: 4.1g   ◎   Carbohydrates: 37.5g   ◎   Protein: 13.8g   ◎   Sugar: 5.3g

cheesy mashed potatoes

Makes 8 cups.

INGREDIENTS

- 6 medium potatoes
- 6 c. frozen cauliflower
- ⅓ c. fat-free Greek yogurt
- 4 wedges Laughing Cow® Light Garlic & Herb Cheese
- ¼ to ½ tsp. garlic powder skim milk
- 2 Tbsp. Parmesan cheese salt and pepper to taste

INSTRUCTIONS

1. Peel potatoes (can leave skins on if desired), cut in half and boil in salted water until tender.
2. Microwave cauliflower according to package directions until very tender.
3. Drain cooked potatoes, add cauliflower, yogurt, cheese, garlic powder. Beat with mixer until it has a creamy consistency. Add a splash of skim milk if mixture is too thick.
4. Salt and pepper to taste.

Nutritional Value
Nutritional information is based on ½ cup.

Calories: 62 ❀ Fat: .4g ❀ Carbohydrates: 10.6g ❀ Protein: 2.5g ❀ Sugar: 1.6g

butternut squash fries

Makes 2 servings.

INGREDIENTS

1   medium butternut squash
    salt
    chili powder
    cooking spray

INSTRUCTIONS

1. Preheat oven to 425 degrees.
2. Peel squash with potato peeler. Cut into quarters. Scoop out seeds.
3. Use crinkle-cut potato cutter to cut ¼-inch slices.
4. Spray cookie sheet with cooking spray and layer fries in single layer.
5. Sprinkle with salt and chili powder to taste.
6. Bake in oven for 30 to 40 minutes until crisp. Flip fries half way through baking.

"Not to be confused with 'Better-Not' Squash Fries! Now you can indulge, sans the greasy fingers and fat! This is a great side to any lunch or dinner."

Nutritional Value
Nutritional information is based on ½ of the fries.

Calories: 100   ❁   Fat: 0g   ❁   Carbohydrates: 20g   ❁   Protein: 2.5g   ❁   Sugar: 5g

butternut squash soufflé

Makes 6 cups.

INGREDIENTS

4 c. cubed butternut squash, peeled
¼ to ⅓ c. sugar-free or natural maple-flavored syrup
3 egg whites
⅛ to ¼ tsp. cayenne pepper
  pinch of cinnamon
¼ c. pecan pieces
  salt and pepper

INSTRUCTIONS

1. Preheat oven to 350 degrees.
2. Peel and cube butternut squash. Cook in microwave on high
   for 6 to 8 minutes or until squash is tender.
3. Add remaining ingredients, except egg whites, and beat with mixer until creamy.
4. In separate bowl, beat egg whites until soft peaks form. Gently fold egg whites
   into squash mixture, ⅓ of egg white mixture at a time. Salt and pepper to taste.

Nutritional Value
Nutritional information is based on ½ cup.

Calories: 44.7 🌼 Fat: 1.8g 🌼 Carbohydrates: 4.8g 🌼 Protein: 1.8g 🌼 Sugar: 1.1g

sweet potato soufflé

Makes 5 cups.

INGREDIENTS

  6   large sweet potatoes
1½ c. low-fat buttermilk
 ¼ c. honey
  4 Tbsp. light butter
  5 egg whites
 ½ tsp. cinnamon
10 packets stevia or ⅓ c. sugar
 ¼ tsp. nutmeg
 ½ tsp. chili powder
 ¼ tsp. crushed red pepper flakes
 ¼ c. chopped pecans
 ¼ c. sugar-free maple syrup (optional)

INSTRUCTIONS

1. Preheat oven to 350 degrees.
2. Cook sweet potatoes in microwave until soft (about 15 minutes).
3. Slice sweet potatoes in half lengthwise, scoop potato out of skins and into a cooking pot. Heat on medium heat.
4. Add buttermilk, honey, butter, cinnamon, nutmeg, chili powder, red pepper flakes and maple syrup (optional).
5. Mash warm potato mixture or beat with hand mixer for creamier consistency.
6. In separate bowl, beat egg whites with mixer until soft peaks form and gently fold into potato mixture.
7. Transfer to casserole dish, sprinkle with chopped pecans and bake for 20 to 25 minutes or until egg whites are set.

> "So light, yet so full of flavor! I love that I don't feel weighed down after eating this. Thanksgiving would not be the same without this side. This could almost pass as a dessert with a few marshmallows thrown on top."

hint:

> Don't be concerned about the sugar! The majority of the sugar count comes from the sweet potatoes which naturally have healthy sugars your body uses for energy.

Nutritional Value

Nutritional information is based on ½ cup.

Calories: 152   Fat: 4.8g   Carbohydrates: 27g   Protein: 6.3g   Sugar: 11g

entrees

chicken wellington roll

Makes 4 servings.

INGREDIENTS

- 4   sheets phyllo dough
- 4   4 oz. uncooked, boneless skinless chicken breasts
- ¾   c. finely diced mushrooms
- ¼   c. finely diced water chestnuts
- ½   c. finely diced red onion
- ½   tsp. garlic powder
- 3   oz. fat-free cream cheese
- 2   Tbsp. fat-free Greek yogurt
    salt and pepper to taste
    garlic salt
    butter-flavored cooking spray

INSTRUCTIONS

1. Preheat oven to 375 degrees.
2. Sauté mushrooms, onions, water chestnuts and garlic powder in nonstick cooking pan until onions are caramelized.
3. Add cheese and yogurt. Cook until cheese is melted and mixed well. Salt and pepper to taste.
4. Pound each chicken breast to ¼-inch in thickness. Spread ¼ of mushroom mixture on chicken and roll up breast.
5. Roll out 4 sheets of phyllo dough and quarter them with a pizza cutter. Spray 2 of the quartered sheets with cooking spray. Put 2 more quartered sheets on top of sprayed sheets and spray with cooking spray.
6. Place 1 rolled chicken on sprayed sheets and roll up. Spray top of roll with cooking spray and sprinkle with garlic salt.
7. Place seam-side down on a cookie sheet coated with cooking spray. Bake for 20 minutes or until dough is lightly brown and crisp and chicken is not pink inside.

> *"I love this healthy spin on an old favorite. Talk about an easy way to impress! Anything wrapped in phyllo dough gets an A+ in my book."*

Nutritional Value
Nutritional information is based on 1 roll.

Calories: 215   ❖   Fat: 3.2g   ❖   Carbohydrates: 10.5g   ❖   Protein: 31g   ❖   Sugar: 3.4g

chicken mushroom quesadilla

Makes 2 servings.

INGREDIENTS

- 4 oz. grilled chicken breast, cut into thin strips
- 4 oz. fresh baby bella mushrooms, sliced
- 1 medium sweet onion, sliced
- ½ c. shredded low-fat mozzarella cheese
- ¼ tsp. garlic salt, divided
- 2 Tbsp. salsa verde
- 2 large whole-wheat, low-carb tortilla

INSTRUCTIONS

1. Sauté all ingredients, except tortillas and cheese, in hot, nonstick pan coated with cooking spray until chicken and veggies are tender. Salt and pepper to taste.
2. Put ½ of chicken mixture on ½ of each tortilla.
   Cover each chicken mixture with ½ of cheese.
3. Fold each tortilla over and cook in nonstick pan coated with cooking spray until bottom of tortillas are lightly brown and crisp.
4. Spray top of tortillas with cooking spray and flip them over in the pan.
   Cook for 2 to 4 minutes or until lightly brown and crisp.

"Because we all get the craving at one point or another, be sure to keep the ingredients for this game-day favorite on hand just in 'queso!'... You know you were thinking it!"

Nutritional Value
Nutritional information is based on 1 quesadilla.

Calories: 279   Fat: 9.5g   Carbohydrates: 14.3g   Protein: 30g   Sugar: 4g

greek-marinated chicken breast

Makes 4 servings.

INGREDIENTS

4	4 oz. chicken breasts
1	Tbsp. olive oil
¼	c. balsamic vinegar
1	Tbsp. lemon juice
2	tsp. minced garlic
2	Tbsp. finely diced kalamata olives
2	packets stevia or 1 Tbsp. sugar
¼	tsp. dried oregano
1	tsp. salt

INSTRUCTIONS

1. Put all ingredients into a large plastic bag. Shake/mix ingredients and refrigerate for 1 to 24 hours — the longer the better.
2. Preheat oven to 375 degrees.
3. Remove chicken from bag and put in a baking dish sprayed with nonstick cooking spray.
4. Bake for 25 to 30 minutes or until juice runs clear when chicken is poked with a fork.

"This dish is great served with your favorite salad or with whole-grain orzo and fresh tomato.

Nutritional Value
Nutritional information is based on 1 chicken breast.

Calories: 172   Fat: 6.8g   Carbohydrates: 2.3g   Protein: 25g   Sugar: 2g

chicken enchiladas

Makes 6 servings.

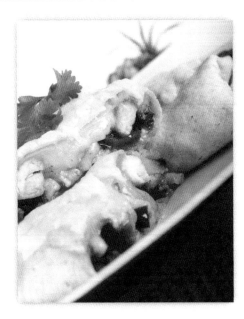

INGREDIENTS

- 1   c. salsa verde
- ⅔   c. low-fat buttermilk
- 1   Tbsp. corn starch
- 2   wedges Laughing Cow® Queso Fresco Cheese
- 2   c. cooked chicken breast, shredded
- 1   c. diced red or sweet onion
- 1   c. fat-free cottage cheese
- 2   oz. low-fat monterey cheese, shredded
- 6   large whole-wheat, low-carb tortilla wraps
- 1   packet stevia or 2 tsp. sugar
- salt and pepper to taste

INSTRUCTIONS

1. Preheat oven to 375 degrees.
2. Sauté onions in nonstick pan until tender. Add cottage cheese, monterey cheese and chicken. Cook until cheese melts and chicken is well blended. Salt and pepper to taste.
3. In separate pan, heat salsa, buttermilk, corn starch, sweetener and Laughing Cow cheese until cheese is melted. Salt and pepper to taste.
4. Fill tortilla with ⅙ of chicken mixture, spread 1 Tbsp. of salsa on chicken and roll tortilla. Repeat with other 5 tortillas. Put in a baking dish sprayed with cooking spray. Cover tortillas with remaining salsa.
5. Bake in oven for 20 to 25 minutes until bubbly and cheese is melted.

"I love these and still can't believe I get to eat them! This is pretty much where all of my favorite things come together — cheese, tortillas and gooey goodness!"

Nutritional Value
Nutritional information is based on 1 enchilada.

Calories: 254   Fat: 6.8g   Carbohydrates: 15g   Protein: 25g   Sugar: 4g

asian-marinated chicken breast

Makes 4 servings.

INGREDIENTS

- 4   4 oz. chicken breasts
- 1   Tbsp. toasted sesame oil
- ¼   c. rice wine vinegar
- 2   Tbsp. low-sodium soy sauce
- 2   tsp. minced garlic
- ¼   tsp. ground ginger
- 2   packets stevia or 1 Tbsp. sugar
- ½   tsp. salt

INSTRUCTIONS

1. Put all ingredients into a large plastic bag. Shake/mix ingredients and refrigerate for 1 to 24 hours — the longer the better.
2. Preheat oven to 375 degrees.
3. Remove chicken from bag and put in a baking dish sprayed with nonstick cooking spray.
4. Bake for 25 to 30 minutes or until juice runs clear when chicken is poked with a fork.
5. Great served with your favorite coleslaw, brown rice and pea pods.

Nutritional Value
Nutritional information is based on 1 chicken breast.

Calories: 167   Fat: 6.5g   Carbohydrates: 0g   Protein: 25g   Sugar: 0g

chicken & mushroom yogurt sauce

Makes 4 servings.

INGREDIENTS

- 4   4 oz. boneless chicken breasts
- 1   c. diced red onion
- 1   Tbsp. minced garlic
- 2   6 oz. cans sliced mushrooms, drained
- ⅔   c. low-sodium, all-natural chicken stock
- 1   6 oz. container fat-free Greek yogurt
- 3   Tbsp. whole-wheat flour, divided
- 1   tsp. Worcestershire sauce
- 1   packet stevia or 2 tsp. sugar

INSTRUCTIONS

1. Put chicken, 2 Tbsp. flour, salt and pepper in plastic bag. Shake until chicken is coated.
2. Brown chicken in a nonstick pan coated with nonstick cooking spray — about 3 minutes per side.
3. Remove chicken and re-spray pan. Sauté onions, mushrooms and garlic until tender.
4. Return chicken to pan, add broth, cover and simmer chicken 20 to 25 minutes or until chicken is no longer pink, and juices run clear when pierced. Remove and place chicken on serving platter and keep warm.
5. Mix 1 Tbsp. flour and Worcestershire sauce with yogurt until well blended.
6. Add yogurt to pan, mix well and simmer until thickened.
7. Pour sauce over chicken. Serve with brown rice or quinoa.

Nutritional Value
Nutritional information is based on 1 chicken breast.

Calories: 222   Fat: 3g   Carbohydrates: 9.5g   Protein: 32g   Sugar: 3g

chicken fingers

Makes 4 servings.

INGREDIENTS

- 1 lb. boneless skinless chicken breast
- ¼ c. fat-free Greek yogurt
- ¼ c. fat-free sour cream
- ¼ c. low-fat buttermilk
- 1 tsp. lemon juice
- 2 tsp. garlic powder, divided
- 1 tsp. onion powder, divided
- ½ tsp. poultry seasoning
- ½ tsp. salt
- ½ c. whole-wheat bread crumbs
  (2-3 slices whole-wheat, low-calorie
  bread ground in food processor)
- ¼ c. whole-grain cornmeal

INSTRUCTIONS

1. Preheat oven to 400 degrees.
2. Cut chicken breasts into 1-by-3-inch strips.
3. Mix yogurt, sour cream, buttermilk, lemon juice, 1 tsp. garlic powder,
   ½ tsp. onion powder and poultry seasoning together, and mix with chicken strips.
4. Mix bread crumbs, cornmeal, 1 tsp. garlic powder and ½ tsp. onion powder together.
5. Coat chicken breast strips in bread crumb mixture and put on baking sheet sprayed
   with cooking spray.
6. Spray chicken strips with cooking spray and bake for 20 minutes.

> "Do we ever really outgrow this kid favorite? It feels so good to know you
> can feed your family something they love while you keep it healthy! Why fry
> your food when you can make it taste even better without all the fat?"

Nutritional Value
Nutritional information is based on 4 chicken strips.

Calories: 218 ❀ Fat: 3g ❀ Carbohydrates: 11g ❀ Protein: 31g ❀ Sugar: 3g

italian-marinated chicken breast

Makes 4 servings.

INGREDIENTS

- 4   4 oz. boneless chicken breasts
- 1   Tbsp. olive oil
- ¼   c. red wine vinegar
- 1   tsp. Italian seasoning
- 2   tsp. minced garlic
- ¼   tsp. crushed red pepper
- 2   packets stevia or 1 Tbsp. sugar
- 1   tsp. salt

INSTRUCTIONS

1. Put all ingredients into a large plastic bag. Shake/mix ingredients and refrigerate for 1 to 24 hours — the longer the better.
2. Preheat oven to 375 degrees.
3. Remove chicken from bag and put in a baking dish sprayed with nonstick cooking spray.
4. Bake for 25 to 30 minutes or until juice runs clear when chicken is poked with a fork.

"This chicken is great served on top of your favorite salad or with a side of whole-grain rice and grilled veggies."

Nutritional Value
Nutritional information is based on 1 chicken breast.

Calories: 167   Fat: 6.5g   Carbohydrates: 0g   Protein: 25g   Sugar: 0g

peachy cream chicken

Makes 4 servings.

INGREDIENTS

4	4 oz. boneless skinless chicken breasts
2	Tbsp. whole-wheat flour
1	tsp. olive oil
1	12 oz. bag frozen, sliced peaches, thawed
1	small red onion, thinly sliced
½	c. diced green pepper
¾	c. low-sodium chicken broth
¼	c. fat-free Greek yogurt
½	tsp. grated lemon peel
2	packets stevia or 1 Tbsp. sugar
6	large basil leaves, rolled up and thinly sliced
¼	tsp. cayenne pepper
	salt and pepper to taste

INSTRUCTIONS

1. Sprinkle chicken breast with flour. Salt and pepper breasts to taste.
2. Add olive oil to nonstick skillet. Add chicken to skillet and cook on medium heat, turning once until chicken is cooked thoroughly (about 15 minutes). Transfer cooked chicken to serving platter and keep warm.
3. Add remaining ingredients (except for sliced basil, lemon peel and yogurt) to skillet and bring to boil.
4. Turn down heat and simmer. Stir frequently until sauce has thickened (about 3 to 5 minutes).
5. Remove sauce from heat and stir in yogurt, lemon and basil. Salt and pepper to taste.
6. Spoon over chicken and serve immediately.

Great served over quinoa or brown rice.

Nutritional Value

Nutritional information is based on 1 chicken breast and ¼ of sauce.

Calories: 210   Fat: 4.8g   Carbohydrates: 9.7g   Protein: 27.8g   Sugar: 5g

tandoori chicken

Makes 4 servings.

INGREDIENTS

4   4 oz. boneless, skinless chicken breasts
2   limes
1   6 oz. container fat-free Greek yogurt
2   Tbsp. low-fat mayo
½   tsp. each ground ginger, garlic powder
    and onion powder
1   tsp. each ground coriander
    and ground cumin
1   Tbsp. smokey paprika
¼   tsp. cayenne pepper
    salt and pepper to taste

INSTRUCTIONS

1. Mix yogurt, mayo, juice of 2 limes and all the spices in a large plastic bag.
    Add chicken and marinate for 1 hour to 24 hours — the longer the better.
2. Preheat oven to 425 degrees.
3. Put chicken and marinade in roasting pan and bake for 30 minutes or
    until juices run clear when thickest part of breast is pierced with a fork.

Nutritional Value
Nutritional information is based on 1 chicken breast.

Calories: 167.2   Fat: 3.5g   Carbohydrates: 5.2g   Protein: 29.3g   Sugar: 2.5g

chicken pizzaioli

Makes 4 servings.

INGREDIENTS

- 4   4 oz. boneless, skinless chicken breasts
- 1   small diced red onion
- 1   28 oz. can crushed tomatoes
- 1½ tsp. dried Italian seasoning
- 1   tsp. garlic salt
- ½   to 1 tsp. red pepper flakes
- 1   tsp. fennel seed
- 2   Tbsp. chopped fresh basil
- 2   packets stevia or 2 Tbsp. sugar
- ¾   c. grated low-fat mozzarella cheese
  salt and pepper to taste

INSTRUCTIONS

1. Preheat oven to 375 degrees.
2. Pound chicken into ½-inch cutlets. Season both sides of cutlets with salt and pepper.
3. Spray oven-safe skillet with cooking spray. Put cutlets in hot skillet and cook for 2 minutes until browned. Flip chicken and brown other side for 2 minutes. Remove chicken.
4. In same pan, sauté onions until soft. Add remaining ingredients (except for cheese and basil) and simmer for 3 minutes. Remove from heat and stir in basil.
5. Transfer chicken to top of tomato mixture. Sprinkle top of cutlets with cheese and bake for 15 to 20 minutes until chicken is thoroughly cooked and cheese is melted.

Goes great with crusty whole-grain Artisan bread and a light salad.

> *"I love Italian food so this meal makes my belly very happy! If I have to have a little whole-wheat pasta this is a great topper for that. I fill up on the veggies and chicken and keep my starchy side smaller."*

Nutritional Value

Nutritional information is based on 1 chicken breast and ¼ of sauce.

Calories: 256.8 ❖ Fat: 6.4g ❖ Carbohydrates: 10.4g ❖ Protein: 32.5g ❖ Sugar: 7.2g

maple pecan chicken

Makes 4 servings.

INGREDIENTS

4   4 oz. boneless, skinless chicken breasts
2   Tbsp. sugar-free or natural maple syrup
¼   c. pecans
¾   c. Busy Girl Healthy Life™
     Whole-Wheat Bread Crumbs, *pg. 97*
¼   tsp. cayenne pepper
     salt and pepper to taste

INSTRUCTIONS

1. Preheat oven to 400 degrees.
2. Pound chicken breasts to ¼-inch thickness.
3. Brush chicken with maple syrup.
4. Finely grind pecans in food processor or blender.
5. In a plastic bag, mix pecans, bread crumbs, cayenne pepper and salt. Add chicken to bread mixture and shake to completely cover chicken.
6. Put chicken on baking sheet sprayed with nonstick cooking spray. Spray top of chicken with cooking spray.
7. Bake in oven for 20 to 25 minutes or until chicken is thoroughly cooked.

> *"Chicken is a staple in so many households, and I believe in keeping it interesting at all times! Nothing like maple and pecans to make this dish irresistible."*

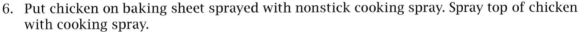
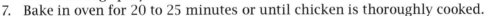

Nutritional Value
Nutritional information is based on 1 chicken breast.

Calories: 210   ❋   Fat: 8.2g   ❋   Carbohydrates: 4.7g   ❋   Protein: 27.2g   ❋   Sugar: <1g

mediterranean chicken

Makes 4 servings.

INGREDIENTS

  8   small boneless, skinless chicken thighs
  2   Tbsp. whole-wheat flour
  1   small diced red onion
  ¼   c. kalamata olives, coarsely chopped
  1   15 oz. can petite diced tomatoes
  ½   c. low-sodium chicken broth
  ½   tsp. dried oregano
  ½   tsp. dried basil
  ½   tsp. garlic powder
  1   packet stevia or 2 tsp. sugar
1½   Tbsp. balsamic vinegar
       salt and pepper to taste

INSTRUCTIONS

1. Sprinkle chicken thighs with flour.
2. Put chicken in a large nonstick skillet sprayed with cooking spray.
3. Brown chicken on both sides, remove from skillet.
4. Add onion to skillet and cook until caramelized.
5. Add tomatoes, olives, chicken broth, vinegar and spices. Stir well.
6. Return chicken to skillet and cook on high until boiling.
7. Reduce heat to low, cover and simmer for 25 to 30 minutes or until chicken is cooked thoroughly (occasionally spooning olive mixture over chicken).

Great served over quinoa or brown rice.

"Never eat bland chicken again! My mouth is watering just thinking about how savory this recipe is. Serve this over your favorite grain or on a bed of greens. Try a side of the Busy Girl Healthy Life™ Greek Dressing (pg. 36) to really wow your taste buds!"

Nutritional Value
Nutritional information is based on 1 chicken breast and ¼ of olive mixture.

Calories: 220.6 ❀ Fat: 8.8g ❀ Carbohydrates: 8.9g ❀ Protein: 22.5g ❀ Sugar: 4.1g

stuffed cran-apple turkey roll

Makes 16 to 20 servings.

INGREDIENTS

1	c. diced celery
1	c. diced onion
1	8 oz. can water chestnuts, drained and diced
2	5 oz. cans mushrooms, drained and diced
1½	c. herb stuffing croutons
1½	to 2 c. low-sodium chicken stock
2	medium crisp apples, cored and diced
¼	c. dried cranberries
¼	c. diced walnuts
2	Tbsp. light butter
2	1½ lb. boneless skinless turkey breasts

INSTRUCTIONS

1. Preheat oven to 375 degrees.
2. Mix celery, onion, water chestnuts, mushrooms, stuffing croutons, apples, cranberries and walnuts together in large mixing bowl.
3. Warm chicken stock and butter in microwave until butter melts.
4. Add chicken stock to crouton mixture and mix thoroughly. Salt and pepper to taste. Let set until croutons are soft and cooled.
5. Pound both turkey breasts to ¼-inch thickness.
6. Put 2 cups stuffing on each turkey breast and roll tightly. Tie each breast with kitchen string (about 6 strings per breast). Spray top of turkey breast with cooking spray.
7. Put turkey breasts in roasting pan and roast in oven for 30 to 35 minutes or until turkey is thoroughly cooked.
8. Let breasts set for a few minutes. Remove string from breasts. Slice each breast into 8 to 10 slices.

Nutritional Value

Nutritional information is based on ¹⁄₁₆ of recipe.

Calories: 141   Fat: 3g   Carbohydrates: 8.9g   Protein: 16.6g   Sugar: 4.6g

santa fe wrap

Makes 7 servings.

INGREDIENTS

1 lb. diced, cooked chicken breast
1 15 oz. can black beans,
    drained and rinsed
1 c. diced red bell pepper
½ c. diced sweet onion
1 c. corn
1 10 oz. can diced tomato
    with green chilies, drained
6 oz. fat-free Greek yogurt
⅔ c. salsa verde
    juice of 1 lime
4 packets stevia or 3 Tbsp. sugar
    salt and pepper to taste
7 large whole-wheat tortilla wraps
    or Joseph's® Lavash Bread

INSTRUCTIONS

1. Combine all ingredients in a large bowl and
   mix well until all ingredients are blended.
2. Put 1 c. of chicken salad in a tortilla wrap, and enjoy!

"For an extra special treat, spread 1 slice of ripe avocado on the wrap and then add the Santa Fe salad. You also can try serving on a bed of romaine or shredded lettuce if you don't want to have the wrap."

Nutritional Value
Nutritional information is based on 1 cup of salad and 1 large tortilla wrap.

Calories: 270   Fat: 5g   Carbohydrates: 20g   Protein: 29g   Sugar: 5.5g

mushroom swiss burger

Makes 5 servings.

INGREDIENTS

- 1 lb. ground turkey (93/7)
  or ground sirloin (93/7)
- 6 oz. chopped portobello mushrooms
- ½ c. diced onion
- 5 wedges of Laughing Cow® Light Swiss
  Cheese (partially frozen for easy chopping)
- 1 to 1½ Tbsp. Worcestershire sauce
- ¼ tsp. garlic powder
  salt and pepper to taste

INSTRUCTIONS

1. Dice frozen cheese.
2. Sauté mushrooms in nonstick skillet until lightly brown.
3. Mix all ingredients together and make into 5 equal patties.
4. Grill until patties are completely cooked through. Serve on your favorite whole-grain hamburger bun or English muffin.

"This is a serious sandwich that will make any burger-lover a believer! Such a fun spin on grilling out!"

Nutritional Value
Nutritional information is based on 1 patty.

Calories: 189.8 ❀ Fat: 7.9g ❀ Carbohydrates: 3.9g ❀ Protein: 20g ❀ Sugar: 2.2g

sloppy turkey joes

Makes 7 cups (21 servings).

INGREDIENTS

2½ lbs. ground turkey (93/7)
1 c. each finely diced red onion, bell pepper, celery, carrots and mushrooms
1 29 oz. can all-natural tomato sauce
½ tsp. each garlic powder and onion powder
1 tsp. Mrs. Dash® All-Natural Table Blend Seasoning
1 tsp. liquid smoke
2 tsp. Worcestershire sauce
2 packets stevia or 1 Tbsp. sugar
salt and pepper to taste

INSTRUCTIONS

1. Brown ground turkey and all the diced vegetables in large nonstick frying pan until turkey is thoroughly cooked and there is no pink left. Salt and pepper to taste.
2. Add the rest of the ingredients and simmer for 20 minutes.
3. Serve on low-calorie, whole-wheat hamburger buns or English muffins.

"These bring back so may memories of being a kid! I'm pretty sure I ate these at every family picnic and also wore them home on my shirt. Try these with the Butternut Squash Fries (pg. 48)!"

Nutritional Value

Nutritional information is based on ⅓ cup.

Calories: 99.8   Fat: 3.8g   Carbohydrates: 4.3g   Protein: 11g   Sugar: 2.2g

greek turkey burger

Makes 5 servings.

INGREDIENTS

  1 lb. ground turkey or ground beef (93/7)

¼ c. finely diced kalamata olives

¼ c. finely diced green olives with pimento

¼ c. diced onion

¼ c. chopped walnuts

¼ c. fat-free feta cheese

¼ tsp. each of garlic powder, dried oregano
and dried dill weed
salt and pepper to taste

INSTRUCTIONS

1. Mix all ingredients together and make into 5 equal patties.
2. Grill until patties are completely cooked through.
3. Serve on your favorite whole-grain hamburger bun or English muffin.
   Mix together fat-free Greek yogurt, a pinch of dried oregano and dill weed
   for a delicious topping for the burger.
4. Top off with a slice of tomato.

> *"This mouth-watering burger is enough to bring a tear to my eye! I have a true love for olives. So this combination is heaven on a bun!"*

Nutritional Value
Nutritional information is based on 1 patty.

Calories: 201.4   Fat: 11.6g   Carbohydrates: 4.7g   Protein: 19.3g   Sugar: <1g

italian turkey burger

Makes 4 to 5 servings.

INGREDIENTS

1   tsp. fennel, chopped or crushed
1   Tbsp. minced garlic
16 oz. ground turkey/chicken/beef
½   c. chopped onions
½   c. fresh parsley or 1 Tbsp. dried parsley
½   c. chopped mushrooms
3   egg whites
½   c. Busy Girl Healthy Life™ Whole-Wheat Bread Crumbs, *pg. 97*
    salt and pepper to taste
¼   tsp. red pepper
1   tsp. Italian seasoning
    If desired for topping — light ricotta cheese,
    slice of light mozzarella or asiago cheese

INSTRUCTIONS

1. Pre-heat the grill.
2. Mix all ingredients together and form 4 to 5 patties.
3. Dance in place while burgers are grilling to burn extra calories.
4. For extra flavor, add low-sugar pizza sauce and 1 Tbsp. asiago cheese,
    slice light mozzarella or a dollop of light ricotta to patty while warm.
5. Serve on buns of choice (try Ezekiel® Buns) and bam! Italian burgers.

> *"Have it your way! Fabulous with toppings or alone.
> The flavors are drool worthy!"*

Nutritional Value
Nutritional information is based on 1 burger.

Calories: 206   Fat: 8g   Carbohydrates: 3.6g   Protein: 25.5g   Sugar: 1.3g

italian turkey sausage

Makes 5 servings.

INGREDIENTS

16 oz. lean ground turkey
2 tsp. olive oil, if desired
½ tsp. garlic powder
3 Tbsp. Italian seasoning
3 Tbsp. fennel seed
½ tsp. red pepper flakes
2 tsp. smokey paprika
¼ tsp. ground cayenne pepper (optional)
   salt and pepper to taste

INSTRUCTIONS

1. Heat olive oil in a frying pan. Add the ground turkey and all seasonings.
2. Cook until well done. Chop turkey while frying to hamburger consistency.

"This was the very first Busy Girl recipe on the website! It is an absolute staple in my house every week. It's also one of my ultimate favorite things to eat and is the base of many recipes I make. Keep this in your house and toss it into anything you can think of to add some lean protein and hefty flavor! Everyone loves this recipe!"

hint:

This recipe can be doubled or tripled, packaged in desired serving sizes and frozen. Can use this low-calorie, low-fat recipe in place of any ground sausage in any recipe.

Nutritional Value

Nutritional information is based on ½ cup.

Calories: 106 ❀ Fat: 16g ❀ Carbohydrates: <1g ❀ Protein: 17g ❀ Sugar: <1g

turkey chili

Makes 10 servings.

INGREDIENTS

- 2 lbs. ground turkey
- 1 medium diced onion
- 1 Tbsp. minced garlic
- 1 28 oz. can crushed tomatoes
- 2 15 oz. cans diced tomatoes with chilies
- 4 Tbsp. tomato paste
- 1 bottle of light beer
- 15 oz. can beef broth
- 2 Tbsp. each of ground cumin and chili powder
- 1 tsp. each of cocoa powder and dried oregano
- 2 bay leaves
- 7 packets stevia or ¼ c. sugar
- 2 15 oz. cans great northern or navy beans
- 4 oz. whole-wheat spaghetti – broken into 2-inch pieces and cooked (feel free to sub your favorite healthy pasta or brown rice)
  salt and pepper to taste

INSTRUCTIONS

1. Brown ground turkey and onions until turkey is fully cooked.
   Add garlic and cook 1 minute more.
2. Add beer, crushed tomatoes, diced tomatoes with chilies, tomato paste, beef broth, bay leaves, cumin, chili powder, cocoa and oregano. Mix well. Stir in beans, cooked spaghetti and sweetener.
3. Simmer for 30 minutes. Remove bay leaves.

hint:

The secret to great chili is to build a multi-level of flavor. The beer and cocoa powder add a wonderfully complex flavor combined with the rest of the ingredients. This chili is tasty, healthy, low calorie and filling! This chili goes wonderfully with sweet corn bread. (See Sweet Corn Bread recipe at www.busygirlhealthylife.com/recipes.)

Nutritional Value

Nutritional information is based on 1½ cup.

Calories: 309 • Fat: 7g • Carbohydrates: 22g • Protein: 24g • Sugar: 7g

chinese casserole

Makes 6 servings.

INGREDIENTS

¾ c. brown rice, uncooked
2 c. low-sodium beef broth
1 lb. ground turkey (93/7)
1 c. diced sweet onion
1½ c. diced celery
8 oz. can water chestnuts, diced
2 c. finely shredded cabbage
⅓ to ½ c. low-sodium soy sauce
1 Tbsp. hoisin sauce
2 tsp. toasted sesame oil
½ tsp. garlic powder
    salt and pepper to taste

INSTRUCTIONS

1. Cook rice according to package directions in 1½ c. beef broth.
2. While rice is cooking, brown turkey, celery, onion, water chestnuts and cabbage in a large nonstick frying pan until turkey is cooked through.
3. Add cooked rice to turkey mixture and mix well.
4. Add remaining beef broth, soy sauce, garlic powder, hoisin sauce and sesame oil to casserole. Mix well and cook until liquid is absorbed.

"I am a sucker for this casserole. The only problem I have with it is sharing! This sweet, spicy, crunchy dish covers any craving I'm having!"

Nutritional Value
Nutritional information is based on about 1 cup.

Calories: 265.6   Fat: 6.8g   Carbohydrates: 26.3g   Protein: 17.6g   Sugar: 4.4g

turkey stuffing

Makes 20 servings.

INGREDIENTS

- 2 c. finely diced celery
- 1½ c. finely diced onion
- 2 6.5 oz. cans mushroom stems and pieces, drained and diced
- 8 oz. can water chestnuts, drained and diced
- 6 c. herb-seasoned stuffing bread crumbs
- 1½ c. Busy Girl Healthy Life™ Italian Turkey Sausage, *pg. 71*
- 4 Tbsp. light butter, melted
- ⅔ c. low-fat buttermilk
- 4 c. low-sodium chicken stock
  salt and pepper to taste

INSTRUCTIONS

1. Preheat oven to 350 degrees.
2. Mix all ingredients together. Let sit for 1 hour so all flavors blend.
3. Transfer to a large casserole dish sprayed with nonstick cooking spray.
4. Bake for 45 minutes or until light crust forms on top of casserole.

> *"My holidays never go without this staple! Try it out and see why I don't need a nap after our feast — so delicious and healthy! Great complement to any ham or turkey dish."*

Nutritional Value

Nutritional information is based on ½ cup.

Calories: 87 ❁ Fat: 3.5g ❁ Carbohydrates: 10.5g ❁ Protein: 5.1g ❁ Sugar: 1.7g

veggie stuffing

Makes 20 servings.

INGREDIENTS

1	c. finely diced onion
1½	c. finely diced celery
8	oz. fresh mini bella mushrooms, diced
8	oz. can water chestnuts, drained and diced
2	c. frozen chopped broccoli, thawed
2	c. frozen cauliflower, thawed and diced
1½	c. Busy Girl Healthy Life™ Italian Turkey Sausage, *pg. 71*
1	c. Busy Girl Healthy Life™ Whole-Wheat Bread Crumbs, *pg. 97*
1	c. fat-free cottage cheese
¼	c. grated Parmesan cheese
2	Tbsp. light butter, melted
½	c. low-fat buttermilk
½	tsp. ground poultry seasoning
¼	tsp. garlic powder
1	c. low-sodium chicken stock
	salt and pepper to taste

INSTRUCTIONS

1. Preheat oven to 350 degrees.
2. Mix all ingredients together. Let sit 1 hour so all flavors blend. Transfer to a large casserole dish sprayed with nonstick cooking spray.
3. Bake for 45 minutes or until light crust forms on top of casserole.

Recipe can be cut in half. Freezes well.

> *"This is one of my absolute favorite things to eat! I could eat this as a meal in itself."*

Nutritional Value

Nutritional information is based on about ½ cup.

Calories: 52.9 ❂ Fat: 1.8g ❂ Carbohydrates: 4.4g ❂ Protein: 5.6g ❂ Sugar: 2.1g

skinny pigs in a blanket

Makes 4 servings.

INGREDIENTS

4   sheets phyllo dough
4   smoked turkey sausages, turkey dogs
    or vegetarian dogs
    butter-flavored cooking spray

INSTRUCTIONS

1. Preheat oven to 400 degrees.
2. Roll out 4 sheets of phyllo dough
    and quarter them with a pizza cutter.
3. Spray 2 of the quartered sheets with
    cooking spray. Put 2 more quartered
    sheets on top of sprayed sheets and
    spray top with cooking spray.
4. Place 1 sausage or hot dog in sprayed sheets and roll up. Spray top of roll.
5. Place on a cookie sheet coated with cooking spray. Bake for 10 to 12 minutes
    or until dough is lightly brown and crisp.

Dip in your favorite sauces!

> *"These are a fun, easy appetizer or meal for kids or at
> any party! Try dipping them in one of my dressings in
> the cookbook! Kid tested, husband approved!"*

Nutritional Value
Nutritional information is based on 1 pig in the blanket.

Calories: 143   ❁   Fat: 6.2g   ❁   Carbohydrates: 10g   ❁   Protein: 11g   ❁   Sugar: 2.2g

pumpkin sausage penne

Makes 8 servings.

INGREDIENTS

1	lb. Busy Girl Healthy Life™ Italian Turkey Sausage, (about 2½ cups), *pg. 71*
1	medium diced onion
2	Tbsp. minced garlic
4	oz. canned sliced mushrooms
¾	c. white wine
1	c. chicken broth
15	oz. can plain pumpkin
¼	tsp. each ground sage and dried thyme
½	c. low-fat buttermilk
12	oz. box whole-wheat penne, cooked
⅓	c. grated Parmesan cheese

INSTRUCTIONS

1. In large pan, sauté mushrooms and onions until onions are translucent.
2. Add garlic and cook for one more minute. Add cooked turkey sausage, white wine, chicken broth, pumpkin, sage, thyme, nutmeg and stir.
3. Add buttermilk, cheese and cooked penne. Mix well.
4. Simmer on low heat for 15 minutes.

"This is my 'fool your husband into eating healthy' dish! He will never know it's not the rich restaurant alternative! Keep your heart and stomach happy."

hint:
Try subbing 12 oz. cooked spaghetti squash for a cleaner dish.

Nutritional Value

Nutritional information is based on about ⅛ of pasta dish.

Calories: 275 ❊ Fat: 5g ❊ Carbohydrates: 32g ❊ Protein: 19g ❊ Sugar: 5g

blue cheese-crusted tenderloin fillet

Makes 4 servings.

INGREDIENTS

4   4 oz. tenderloin fillets
⅓   c. low-fat crumbled blue cheese
½   c. Busy Girl Healthy Life™
     Whole-Wheat Bread Crumbs, *pg. 97*
¼   tsp. garlic salt
⅛   tsp. cayenne pepper
1   Tbsp. chopped fresh basil
     salt and pepper to taste

INSTRUCTIONS

1. Preheat oven to 450 degrees.
2. Combine cheese, bread crumbs,
   garlic salt, cayenne and basil in mixing bowl. Set aside.
3. Spray oven-proof skillet with cooking spray. Generously season fillets with
   salt and pepper.
4. Sear first side of steak for about 2 minutes until well browned. Flip steak
   and top each with ¼ of cheese mixture pressing gently into meat.
5. Put steaks in oven and bake for 6 to 7 minutes or until they feel firm but springy
   to the touch. Steaks should be medium rare. If medium is desired cook steaks for
   another 1 to 2 minutes. Cheese mixture will be lightly browned and crusted.
6. Let steaks rest for a few minutes before serving.

Nutritional Value
Nutritional information is based on 1 fillet.

Calories: 203   ❋   Fat: 8.7g   ❋   Carbohydrates: 2.1g   ❋   Protein: 27g   ❋   Sugar: <1g

philly cheesesteak quesadilla

Makes 2 servings.

INGREDIENTS

- 4 oz. raw tenderloin, cut into thin strips
- 4 oz. fresh baby bella mushrooms, sliced
- 1 medium sweet onion, sliced
- 1 medium red bell pepper, sliced
- ½ c. shredded, low-fat mozzarella cheese
- ¼ tsp. garlic salt, divided
  pinch of dried thyme leaves
- 2 large whole-wheat, low-carb tortilla

INSTRUCTIONS

1. In a hot, nonstick pan coated with nonstick cooking spray, sauté all ingredients, except tortillas and cheese, until steak and veggies are tender. Salt and pepper to taste.
2. Put ½ of steak mixture on ½ of each tortilla. Cover each steak mixture with ½ of cheese.
3. Fold each tortilla over and cook in nonstick pan coated with cooking spray until bottom of tortillas are lightly brown and crisp.
4. Spray top of tortillas with cooking spray and flip them over in the pan. Cook for 2 to 4 minutes or until that side is lightly brown and crisp.

Nutritional Value
Nutritional information is based on 1 tortilla.

Calories: 278 ❋ Fat: 10g ❋ Carbohydrates: 16g ❋ Protein: 29g ❋ Sugar: 5g

pork tenderloin chops

Makes 4 servings.

INGREDIENTS

4   4 oz. boneless pork
    tenderloin chops
½   c. low-fat buttermilk
1   c. Busy Girl Healthy Life™
    Whole-Wheat Bread Crumbs, *pg. 97*
2   tsp. dijon mustard
¼   tsp. each garlic powder,
    onion powder and ground sage
    salt and pepper to taste

INSTRUCTIONS

1. Preheat oven to 375 degrees.
2. Marinate tenderloins in buttermilk and mustard for 1 hour or overnight.
3. Mix bread crumbs with garlic powder, onion powder and sage.
4. Dredge tenderloins in bread crumbs and put on a baking sheet sprayed with
   cooking spray. Salt and pepper to taste. Spray top of tenderloins with cooking spray.
5. Bake in oven for 20 to 25 minutes, or until light pink inside, flipping chops halfway
   through baking time.

Nutritional Value
Nutritional information is based on 1 chop.

Calories: 181   Fat: 4.4g   Carbohydrates: 6g   Protein: 27.2g   Sugar: 2.5g

fish & seafood

cayenne lime shrimp

Makes about 31 to 40 servings.

INGREDIENTS

- 1 lb. (31-40 count) frozen raw shrimp, thawed, peeled and deveined
- 2 Tbsp. lime juice
- 2 tsp. light olive oil
- ½ tsp. cayenne pepper
- ½ tsp. garlic salt

INSTRUCTIONS

1. Rinse shrimp. Combine all ingredients and marinate in refrigerator for 30 minutes.
2. Remove shrimp from marinade and grill 2 to 3 minutes on each side until shrimp is tender and cooked through. Do not over cook.

"Throw another shrimp on the barbie! These shrimp are the perfect party starter, and also go perfectly on any skewer or salad."

Nutritional Value
Nutritional information is based on 1 cooked shrimp.

Calories: 10.6   Fat: .3g   Carbohydrates: 0g   Protein: 1.9g   Sugar: 0g

coconut shrimp

Makes 31-40 coconut shrimp.

INGREDIENTS

- 1 lb. (31-40 count) frozen, shelled and deveined raw shrimp, thawed
- 1 c. panko bread crumbs
- ½ c. unsweetened shredded coconut
- ½ Busy Girl Healthy Life™ Whole-Wheat Bread Crumbs, *pg. 97*
- 3 egg whites
- ¼ tsp. cayenne pepper
- 2 packets stevia or 1 Tbsp. sugar
- 2 to 3 Tbsp. water
  salt and pepper to taste

INSTRUCTIONS

1. Preheat oven to 375 degrees.
2. Put flour, salt and pepper in large plastic bag. Shake bag. Add shrimp and shake until shrimp is coated with flour.
3. Put panko, coconut, cayenne, sweetener, salt and pepper in a large shallow bowl and mix well.
4. In separate bowl, whisk egg whites with water.
5. Working with a few shrimp at a time, dip floured shrimp in egg wash. Then put shrimp into coconut mixture and roll around until shrimp are thoroughly covered.
6. Place breaded shrimp on nonstick baking sheet and bake for 10 minutes or until shrimp are firm and cooked through.

Goes great with jalapeño coconut rice.

Asian Dipping Sauce:
Whisk 2 Tbsp. Asian sweet chili dipping sauce with 2 Tbsp. low-sodium chicken sauce for a tasty addition — only 45 Calories!

Nutritional Value
Nutritional information is based on 1 shrimp.

Calories: 37.4   Fat: .6g   Carbohydrates: 3.5g   Protein: 3.7g   Sugar: <1g

asian salmon

Makes 4 servings

INGREDIENTS

- 4   4 oz. skinless salmon
- ⅓   c. low-sodium soy sauce
- ⅓   c. orange juice
- ¼   c. sugar-free or natural maple syrup
- 1   tsp. sesame oil
- ¼   to ½ tsp. ground ginger
- ¼   tsp. garlic powder
     salt and pepper to taste

INSTRUCTIONS

1. Preheat oven to 400 degrees.
2. Mix all ingredients except salmon in oven-proof baking dish.
3. Add salmon and flip in sauce until completely covered. Marinate for 20 minutes.
4. Bake salmon in sauce for 15 to 20 minutes, flipping half way through (periodically basting fillets), until fish is cooked to medium to medium-well depending on preference.
5. Pour any remaining sauce over salmon before serving.

Nutritional Value
Nutritional information is based on 1 fillet.

Calories: 169   Fat: 5.2g   Carbohydrates: 5.5g   Protein: 24.5g   Sugar: 1.8g

crunchy fish sticks

Makes 4 servings.

Makes ¾ c. (12 Tbsp.)

INGREDIENTS

Fish Sticks

1 lb. white fish (haddock, cod, tilapia or flounder)
1 c. Busy Girl Healthy Life™
   Whole-Wheat Bread Crumbs, *pg. 97*
½ c. whole-wheat flour
3 egg whites, beaten
⅛ tsp. each garlic and onion powder
   salt and pepper to taste

Tarter Sauce

½ c. fat-free Greek yogurt
2 Tbsp. low-fat mayo
1 tsp. mustard
2 Tbsp. sweet pickle relish
1 tsp. vinegar
1 packet stevia or 2 tsp. sugar
   salt to taste.

INSTRUCTIONS

1. Preheat oven to 400 degrees.
2. Cut fish into 4- by 1-inch sticks.
3. Put flour into plastic bag, and add salt and pepper to taste.
   Add fish sticks to bag and shake well until sticks are covered with flour.
4. Mix bread crumbs and spices (including salt and pepper), and stir well.
5. Dredge floured sticks in beaten egg whites, then in bread crumb mixture,
   making sure fish is well covered.
6. Place breaded fish sticks on pre-sprayed baking sheet. Bake for 10 to 15 minutes
   until fish is done.
7. Mix tarter sauce ingredients together.
8. Add a splash of skim milk if sauce is too thick.

*"These are so quick and fun to make with your kids!
If you can't have shore lunch, this is the next best thing!"*

Nutritional Value

Nutritional information is based on ¼ of fish sticks (about 4 to 6 sticks).

Calories: 194.3   Fat: 1.25g   Carbohydrates: 13.8g   Protein: 27.5g   Sugar: .8g

Tarter Sauce

Calories: 10.6   Fat: .2g   Carbohydrates: 1.3g   Protein: 1g   Sugar: 1.3g

fish tacos

Makes 8 servings.

INGREDIENTS

1½ lbs. mild white fish
    (haddock, cod, tilapia, etc.)
8   whole-wheat soft tortillas (warmed
    or cooked in frying pan with olive oil
    spray – 1 minute each side)

Marinade

2   Tbsp. fresh lime juice
1   tsp. olive oil
½   tsp. cumin
½   tsp. paprika,
½   tsp. garlic powder)

Coleslaw

1   bag shredded cabbage (about 4 cups)
½   c. chopped green onion
1 to 2 Tbsp. finely chopped jalapeño
1   Tbsp. chopped fresh cilantro
3   Tbsp. white wine vinegar
2   Tbsp. fresh lime juice
1   tsp. celery salt
2   Tbsp. olive oil
3   Tbsp. fat-free Greek yogurt
½   tsp. garlic powder
6   packets stevia or ¼ c. sugar

Cucumber/Corn Salsa

2   c. diced cucumbers
2   finely diced Roma tomatoes
1   c. corn
¼   c. diced green onion
1   Tbsp. finely diced jalapeño
1   Tbsp. chopped fresh cilantro
2   Tbsp. fresh lime juice
½   tsp. ground cumin
½   tsp. garlic powder
2   tsp. olive oil
1   packet stevia or 2 tsp. sugar
    salt and pepper to taste

INSTRUCTIONS

1. Marinate fish in marinade, set aside.
2. Preheat oven to 375 degrees.
3. While fish is marinating, in large bowl beat together white wine vinegar, lime juice, celery salt, olive oil, yogurt, garlic powder and sweetener from coleslaw recipe. Add cabbage, green onion, jalapeño and cilantro. Mix well and set aside.
4. Bake fish for 10 to 12 minutes or until fish is done.
5. While fish is baking, mix together salsa ingredients.
6. When fish is done, pull fish apart with forks to roughly shred. To prepare tacos, put coleslaw in wrap, followed by some fish and top with the salsa.

Nutritional Value
Nutritional information is based on 1 taco.

Calories: 250   Fat: 9g   Carbohydrates: 13g   Protein: 27g   Sugar: 5g

seafood enchiladas

Makes 8 servings.

INGREDIENTS

12	oz. crab diced (can use imitation crab)
12	oz. finely diced cooked shrimp
⅔	c. low-fat buttermilk
1	c. fat-free cottage cheese
1	c. fat-free ricotta cheese
1	c. low-fat monterey cheese, shredded
1	medium red onion
1	Tbsp. corn starch
¾	c. salsa verde, divided
8	whole-wheat, low-carb large tortillas
1	packet stevia or 2 tsp. sugar

INSTRUCTIONS

1. Preheat oven to 375 degrees.
2. Sauté onions, in nonstick pan until tender.
3. Add cottage cheese, monterey cheese, crab, shrimp and ¼ c. salsa verde. Cook until cheese melts and seafood is well blended. Salt and pepper to taste.
4. In separate pan, heat ½ c. salsa, buttermilk, corn starch, sweetener and ricotta cheese until bubbly and cheese is melted. Salt and pepper to taste.
5. Fill tortilla with ⅛ of seafood mixture and roll tortilla. Repeat with other 7 tortillas.
6. Put in a baking dish sprayed with cooking spray. Cover tortillas with salsa mixture.
7. Bake in oven for 20 to 25 minutes until bubbly.

Nutritional Value
Nutritional information is based on 1 enchilada.

Calories: 270   Fat: 7.2g   Carbohydrates: 13.2g   Protein: 32.3g   Sugar: 4.1g

desserts

chocolate cheesecake bites

Makes about 15 servings.

INGREDIENTS

4	oz. fat-free cream cheese
4	oz. fat-free Greek yogurt
15	baked mini phyllo shells
6	packets stevia or ¼ c. sugar
½	tsp. vanilla
1	Tbsp. cocoa powder
	topping of choice or chocolate sprinkles (optional)

INSTRUCTIONS

1. Bring cream cheese and yogurt to room temperature.
2. Beat together cream cheese, yogurt, vanilla, cocoa powder and sweetener until creamy.
3. Fill phyllo shells full with cheese mixture. Sprinkle with chocolate sprinkles if desired.
4. Chill for 1 hour, and enjoy!

hint:

These freeze well. Make lots ahead of time and freeze. When you go to a party, simply take desired amount out of freezer, thaw and people will beg for the recipe! Always keep a supply on hand in the freezer. When you get that urge for something sweet, grab 1 or 2 and you will satisfy that craving without eating a lot of calories or fat.

"I've never met a chocolate dessert I didn't like! This is a party favorite, and aren't they just the cutest darn things? I love that they come in their own edible container and are the perfect bite-sized treat!"

Nutritional Value
Nutritional information is based on 1 cheesecake bite.

Calories: 31   Fat: 1g   Carbohydrates: 2.6g   Protein: 1.9g   Sugar: <1g

chocolate coffee soufflés

Makes about 6 servings.

INGREDIENTS

- ¼ c. unsweetened cocoa powder
- 1 Tbsp. instant coffee granules
- 2 Tbsp. cornstarch
- 1 tsp. ground cinnamon
- 2 packets stevia or 1 Tbsp. sugar
- ½ tsp. cream of tarter
- ¾ c. fat-free evaporated milk
- ½ c. sugar-free or natural maple syrup
- 3 egg whites, room temperature
- 2 egg yolks, room temperature

INSTRUCTIONS

1. Preheat oven to 400 degrees.
2. Coat six 6-ounce soufflé cups with cooking spray. Place cups on baking sheet.
3. In sauce pan, whisk together cocoa powder, instant coffee, cornstarch, sweetener and cinnamon. Stir in milk and maple syrup, and whisk over medium heat until hot (about 4 to 8 minutes).
4. In small bowl, whisk egg yolks lightly. Slowly whisk in ½ c. of cocoa mixture.
5. Pour into the saucepan and mix well.
6. In a large bowl, with an electric mixer, beat egg whites and cream of tartar on high until soft peaks form.
7. Gently stir ⅓ of egg white into cocoa mixture. Fold in remaining egg whites until no white streaks remain. Do not over stir.
8. Evenly divide mixture into prepared cups and bake for 15 to 20 minutes until soufflés are puffed, and a knife inserted in center comes out clean. Serve immediately.

> *"These are perfect for when I am having a crazy chocolate craving! Make sure you have enough people to help you eat these so you don't eat the whole batch!"*

Nutritional Value
Nutritional information is based on 1 soufflé.

Calories: 79   Fat: 1.7g   Carbohydrates: 9.5g   Protein: 5.3g   Sugar: 4g

chewy chocolate brownies

Makes 12 servings.

INGREDIENTS

1¼ c. whole-wheat pastry flour
1½ tsp. baking powder
 ½ tsp. salt
 ⅔ c. sugar-free cocoa powder
16 packets stevia or ¾ c. sugar
 5 oz. fat-free Greek yogurt
 4 oz. fat-free cream cheese, room temperature
 4 oz. carrot baby food
 1 egg + 2 egg whites
 ¼ c. sugar-free or natural maple syrup
 1 tsp. vanilla

INSTRUCTIONS

1. Preheat oven to 375 degrees.
2. Mix together all dry ingredients.
   Beat together all wet ingredients.
   Stir wet ingredients into dry ingredients.
3. Spray 8x11 baking pan. Spread brownie mix in pan.
4. Bake for 20 to 25 minutes or until a knife inserted
   into brownies comes out clean.
5. Let cool. Cut into 12 bars.

"Try these and see if you can fool any brownie lover into choosing this healthier option! Why eat all the extra calories when you can make the sin-free version? I love to cut these into small bites and savor each one."

Nutritional Value
Nutritional information is based on 1 bar.

Calories: 85   Fat: 1g   Carbohydrates: 11.6g   Protein: 3.9g   Sugar: 2.5g

mini carrot cake muffins

Makes 48 mini muffins.

INGREDIENTS

  2   c. whole-wheat flour
1½   c. stevia or 1 c. brown sugar
  ¼   c. olive oil
  ¼   c. applesauce
  ½   c. plain, fat-free Greek yogurt
  2   tsp. cinnamon
  ¼   tsp. sea salt
  2   tsp. baking powder
  2   c. grated carrot
  1   c. crushed pineapple
  1   egg
  3   egg whites
  1   Tbsp. zest of orange
  1   small container Cool Whip®
  1   small container fat-free cream
       cheese (if desired for a creamier
       frosting/topping)

INSTRUCTIONS

1. Preheat oven to 350 degrees. Line mini-muffin tin with paper liners.
2. Beat eggs. Add sugar and oil. Add remaining ingredients. Mix well.
3. Pour into mini-muffin cups. Bake for 20 minutes.
4. Top each muffin with a dollop of Cool Whip and enjoy!

Try whipping ½ c. fat-free cream cheese with 1 cup Fat-Free Cool Whip for a more frosting-like topping. Just add a dollup, and enjoy!

Nutritional Value
Nutritional information is based on 1 muffin.

Calories: 37.9   Fat: 1.5g   Carbohydrates: 1.5g   Protein: 1.4g   Sugar: 1.3g

With Whipped Topping
Calories: 40.4   Fat: 1.5g   Carbohydrates: 1.5g   Protein: 1.4g   Sugar: 1.5g

mini strawberry cheesecake bites

Makes about 15 servings.

INGREDIENTS

- 4 oz. fat-free cream cheese
- 4 oz. fat-free Greek yogurt
- 15 baked mini phyllo shells
- 15 whole strawberries, fresh or frozen
- 7 packets stevia or ¼ c. sugar
- ½ tsp. vanilla
- 1 Tbsp. balsamic vinegar

INSTRUCTIONS

1. Bring cream cheese and yogurt to room temperature. Mix balsamic vinegar and two packets of sweetener (1 Tbsp. sugar). Pour over strawberries and mix well.
2. Beat together cream cheese, yogurt, vanilla and remaining sweetener until creamy.
3. Fill phyllo shells ¾-full with cheese mixture. Put 1 strawberry in shell and gently push down until inserted into cheese mixture.
4. Chill for 1 hour, and enjoy!

hint:

These freeze well. Make lots ahead of time and freeze. When you go to a party, simply take desired amount out of freezer, thaw and people will beg for the recipe! Always keep a supply on hand in the freezer. When you get that urge for something sweet, grab 1 or 2 and you will satisfy that craving without eating a lot of calories or fat.

Nutritional Value
Nutritional information is based on 1 cheesecake bite.

Calories: 32   Fat: 1g   Carbohydrates: 3.2g   Protein: 1.9g   Sugar: 1.5g

maple pumpkin cheesecake

Makes about 9 servings.

INGREDIENTS

12 oz. fat-free cream cheese
½ c. sugar-free or natural maple syrup
½ c. fat-free Greek yogurt or fat-free sour cream
½ tsp. vanilla
2 eggs
2 egg whites
8 oz. canned pumpkin (not pie mix, just plain pumpkin)
¾ to 1 tsp. ground cinnamon
⅛ to ¼ tsp. ground nutmeg

INSTRUCTIONS

1. Preheat oven to 375 degrees.
2. Beat cream cheese and syrup until smooth. Blend in yogurt, vanilla and spices. Beat in eggs one at a time. Beat in egg whites. Blend in pumpkin until smooth.
3. Pour into an 8 x 8 baking dish and bake for about 25 to 30 minutes or until cheesecake is set.
4. Cool and refrigerate for at least 4 hours. Cut into 9 square pieces. You also can cut into 1-inch squares and serve as an appetizer or mini dessert. are puffed, and a knife inserted in center comes out clean. Serve immediately.

Nutritional Value

Nutritional information is based on ⅑ of cheesecake.

Calories: 75.7   Fat: .4g   Carbohydrates: 6.4g   Protein: 8.6g   Sugar: 2.4g

cranberry treat

Makes 6 servings.

INGREDIENTS

- 12 oz. bag frozen cranberries
- ½ c. white wine
- 12 packets stevia or ½ c. sugar
- 1 package unflavored gelatin
- ⅔ c. lukewarm water
- 6 oz. fat-free cream cheese
  pecan pieces (optional)

INSTRUCTIONS

1. Put frozen cranberries in nonstick sauce pan. Add wine and simmer until cranberries burst and are creamy (stirring a few times while simmering).
2. Add gelatin to water and let sit for a few minutes.
3. Remove cranberry mixture from heat and stir in sweetener. Stir in gelatin water and cream cheese. Mix thoroughly.
4. Pour into six ½ c. ramekins. Sprinkle with a few pecan pieces, if desired.
5. Cover and put in refrigerator until cooled and firm. Serve cold.

Nutritional Value
Nutritional information is based on 1 ramekin.

Calories: 76.7   Fat: 0g   Carbohydrates: 63g   Protein: 4.5g   Sugar: 4g miscellaneous

whole-wheat bread crumbs

INGREDIENTS

1   loaf low-calorie, 100% whole-wheat
    bread (I use Healthy Life® bread
    — 35 calories per slice)

INSTRUCTIONS

1. Preheat oven to 350 degrees.
2. Cut crust off of bread. Put in food
   processor or blender, and blend to
   a fine crumb consistency.
3. Spread out on jelly roll pan, and
   spray with olive oil cooking spray.
4. Bake in oven, stirring occasionally, until
   bread crumbs are dry and lightly brown.

hint:

*Freezes well in plastic storage bags. Excellent for all recipes calling for
bread crumbs. You can add garlic salt and Italian seasoning to spice up
the bread crumbs to your liking.*

Nutritional Value
Nutritional information is based on 1 cup.

Calories: 110   Fat: 0g   Carbohydrates: 17g   Protein: 7.9g   Sugar: 3g

parmesan crisps

Makes 16 servings.

INGREDIENTS

 1 c. grated parmesan cheese
 ¼ tsp. garlic powder
 ⅛ tsp. chili powder

INSTRUCTIONS

1. Preheat oven to 350 degrees.
2. Mix spices with Parmesan cheese.
3. Drop 1 Tbsp. of cheese on baking sheet.
4. Bake for 3 to 5 minutes until edges of cheese are lightly brown. Let cool.

"Take any old dish or salad and make it impressive by adding this simple garnish. These are great as an appetizer, too!"

Nutritional Value
Nutritional information is based on 1 crisp.

Calories: 21   Fat: 1.5g   Carbohydrates: 0g   Protein: 2g   Sugar: 0g

whole-wheat croutons

INGREDIENTS

3   slices whole-wheat, low-calorie bread
     cooking spray
¼   tsp. garlic salt
1   Tbsp. grated parmesan cheese

INSTRUCTIONS

1. Preheat oven to 325 degrees.
2. Cut crust off of bread. Cut bread into ½" x ½" cubes.
3. Spread out on jelly roll pan and spray with cooking spray.
4. Sprinkle with garlic salt and parmesan.
5. Bake in oven, stirring occasionally, for 10 to 12 minutes until croutons are dry and lightly brown.
6. Store in air tight container and use on all your salads and soups for that extra crunch!

tip:

Let your taste buds be your guide! Experiment with other herbs and seasonings to change the flavor of the croutons — there are so many options!

Nutritional Value
Nutritional information is based on 1 cup.

Calories: 105   Fat: 0g   Carbohydrates: 17g   Protein: 6g   Sugar: 3g

index

Be sure to visit www.busygirlhealthylife.com
for more fast, fun and easy recipes!

Lori Harder's
busy girl
HEALTHY LIFE

Made in the USA
Lexington, KY
23 October 2012